Business and Religion

BUSINESS
AND RELIGION

A New Depth Dimension in Management

EDITED BY

EDWARD C. BURSK

Editor, *Harvard Business Review*

HARPER & BROTHERS PUBLISHERS, NEW YORK

Contents

Introduction

Has business developed a conscience?

Whether it has or not, individuals in business are becoming increasingly concerned about problems of ethics, morals, and religion. And they are increasingly willing to say so for all to hear, and to discuss their deep worries and their high hopes with all who feel the same, including many of their fellow businessmen. Witness a whole series of meetings, speeches, articles—many of the latter appearing in one of businessmen's own magazines, *Harvard Business Review*.

As the editor of that magazine, I have drawn together some of the most appropriate articles in the belief that, in one handful like this (though more than one mindful), they may gain in usefulness.

I respectfully pose these questions:

Have businessmen become more thoughtful in ethical matters because business itself has changed, or have businessmen become more sensitive and in the process changed business?

Why will businessmen sometimes observe the spirit of an unwritten contract quicker than the word of a written contract?

Have businessmen, perhaps aided by the fact that today they are more managers than owners and therefore have more stake in stability than in immediate profits, simply adopted the long-run view in which moral dealings pay off?

Is there a dividing line between a code of good conduct and a credo of religion—and why do businessmen like to find practical reasons for doing unselfish acts?

Why do businessmen value the dignity of man as something more than a deluxe combination of chemicals and electricity, whether oneself or others?

I also respectfully beg these questions; that is, I do not even dream of trying to answer them. The authors in the following pages are more valiant. In fact some of them have won a citation from The Laymen's Movement for a Christian World: Kenneth E. Boulding, Abram T. Collier, Reinhold Niebuhr, O. A. Ohmann, and Raphael Demos. But it is still up to each reader to find his own answers. More power to him!

As indicated, the chapters of this book originally appeared as articles in the *Harvard Business Review*. Accordingly, thanks are due not only to all the individual authors but to all the members of the *Review* staff who helped prepare them for publication —particularly Miss Virginia B. Fales, Miss Elizabeth H. Knox, Mrs. Janet Bertoni, Mrs. Joyce Lebowitz, and Miss Margery Stern.

E. C. B.

January 1959

Business and Religion

1.

Business and Religion

By James W. Culliton*

Over recent years there has been, I believe, a growing tendency for businessmen to suspect that efficiency solely in things material is not sufficient to justify private enterprise. Many businessmen, applying their fundamental skill of recognizing change and adjusting to it, have been taking certain steps toward treating people more as human beings than as essentially economic entities. The more I observe what these businessmen are striving to achieve, the more I suspect that maybe religion has something to offer business. It is on the basis of such surmise—not knowledge or firm conviction—that I write this article.

Not infrequently I have heard a businessman say, "Now, I am not a religious man, but . . ." and go on to demonstrate that perhaps religion has something to do with his problems. The tone is always apologetic, as if a businessman really should not have such thoughts, or as if religion were something apart from the realities of life and therefore he might be showing some weakness to his fellow man if he harbored any thoughts about religion.

I have frequently wondered if this attitude might not be blinding many businessmen in two important ways:

(1) Might there not be the barest chance that religion, through its cumulated experience, would know some things about men, life, and the

* Mr. Culliton is dean of the Edward N. Hurley College of Foreign and Domestic Commerce, University of Notre Dame.

world which businessmen could use to their own advantage and to the advantage of society?

(2) Is it not true that religion is a fact and therefore part of the total facts with which anyone in an administrative position has to deal?

The issue is complicated by emotions and by various interpretations of the meaning of religion. Yet it is one which seems to me to deserve the conscious attention of businessmen. What they do about it is not at the moment of great concern to me. I do feel, however, that it is worthy of their consideration to do with it what they will. And on quite a few occasions I have found that businessmen agree. For instance, at a meeting I attended the subject came up apparently because the participating businessmen felt that it was appropriate. Let me tell you about that meeting.

THE WORLD'S PROBLEMS

A group of some fifty men had gathered together to discuss the most profitable things which might be done to improve the world. The group was comprised of men interested in business but with many varied backgrounds. It included specialists in marketing, advertising, statistics, labor, economics, production, history—almost anything.

There was no evidence of "the-world-is-going-to-hell, unless . . ." attitude. The group was conscious that the world was facing some mighty important problems—and that mere man was a rather ignorant fellow. There was, however, a fundamental optimism in the air: with continued diligence mere man might be able to do a little better job of making the world a better place in which to live.

Some of the discussions centered around the familiar theme that technical progress has far outstripped our social skills. The inference was that attempts should be made, especially through research, to find ways and means of developing social skills at a more consistent pace.

The cold war did not go unnoticed. Some who felt strongly that the conflict of ideals between democracy and totalitarianism might be a crucial contest stressed the need of finding ways of fostering a broader understanding of what democracy is.

Including Religion

Many general and specific proposals were made in connection with these and other well-known classifications of the problems of today. The role of government in human activities and the function of education received their share of attention. Then, after many minutes and many stirring statements, one man known for his forthrightness and realism—let us call him Mr. Blank—rose somewhat slowly, to say:

"I should like to suggest an area for consideration that I haven't heard mentioned today, even implicitly. I hesitate to bring it up, and yet I feel that I must because I believe that it is very important and should not be overlooked. I haven't said anything until now because, frankly, I have been trying to put into words what I have been thinking and I haven't been able to do it. So I will say imperfectly what I really have in mind.

"We have been talking here this afternoon about the physical sciences, about the social sciences in general and some of them in particular. And yet we haven't mentioned one very important area of human activities— religion. I do not mean Religion with a capital R, or any particular sect or creed, and I don't think I mean the Church, with or without a capital. Yet, as I read history, as I observe the facts of life today, I cannot help but see that religion—or some spiritual force—is, in fact, part of the realities of life. I don't quite see how we can discuss the world's problems without recognizing it.

"We have had many proposals this afternoon for research into this and that; but does anyone really know the part that religion has played, can play, or ought to play in the general scheme of things?"

There was an obvious reaction. Several persons clamored to speak. One who succeeded in getting a hearing said:

"I am glad that this point was raised. I, too, have been trying to put into words something very close to what has just been said. I feel that religion—or call it what you will—not only is a real fact which ought to be included in our observation but also has powers and potentialities with which both the scholars and practical men are only vaguely familiar. I think that, if we were able to dispense with some of the emotions that show up whenever someone mentions religion and to look more closely at what it is, in contrast to what some people think it ought to be, we might be surprised at the results."

It was generally agreed, I believe, that the subject was important, that it was worthy of consideration. Yet, so far as I could tell, no one quite knew what to do about it in a practical sort of way. I do not know either, but the purpose of this article is to explore, unpretentiously, some of the implications of the thought that religion may have something to do with the world and its problems, and in fact with the problems of business administration.

BASIC MISUNDERSTANDING

My first approach is a negative one. Mr. Blank, the same gentleman who had introduced the question of religion into the discussion, later, in a luncheon conversation, reported part of a prayer that he had heard a minister give: "Oh Lord, deliver us from lying called propaganda and from plunder called profits!" This led several others to a discussion of what they considered to be the appalling lack of understanding on the part of the ministry of the real nature of the problems of business and of the workings of our economic system. Many of those present cited instance after instance where ministers of the church criticized the actions of businessmen because (the businessmen said) "they did not understand."

Quite naturally, this type of discussion leads to the question of what can be done about such situations. So far as I have been able to observe, the first (and usually the last) answer is to suggest that the candidates for the ministry should receive better education in business. "They should know better."

Some of my acquaintances have in fact acted in a small way to make it possible for members of the ministry "to know better," through sponsoring and participating in group discussions at their churches or through helping to see that the minister's training program included some things in this area. I believe, however, that there is something basically inadequate in such schemes no matter how effective they appear to be on the surface. It is that they are essentially defensive. Indeed, many times the businessman who advocates them has an attitude of righteous smugness. His position is: "I am misunderstood." Either he does nothing about it except "cry in his beer," or he takes steps to do what he can to see that *his* position is better understood.

Only rarely have I been able to discover even a trace of the possible suspicion that "maybe the minister has something there." Is it absolutely necessary that the minister is an ignorant fellow, so engrossed in his prayers and the cloth that he does not know anything about what is going on in the world? Isn't there an outside chance that this man—dealing as he does almost exclusively with people—has learned a little bit about life or about what some people, other than businessmen, see in life and want from life?

If the businessman ever harbored these suspicions, he might be on the verge of discovering in a very useful way what I think our friend at the "world's problems" meeting was searching for. Do there have to be two worlds—religion and business? Isn't there something that religion has to offer that can be merged with business, in a sense much more fundamental than factories holding prayer meetings? It looks to me as if maybe religion does have something business could use, and lately I have seen two hopeful clues.

Concept of Charity

The first clue is found in the growing currency of the phrase "business responsibility." Donald K. David, who was active in popularizing this term when he was dean of the Harvard Business School, has recognized that it is inadequate as long as it is a mere generalization. His first major attempt to explore the term suggested a further twofold breakdown of this responsibility of business and businessmen. After pointing out that "as a first objective, the competent business administrator must furnish society with material satisfactions," he went on to say:

The second objective which the competent business administrator must recognize and willingly accept is an even greater responsibility. We all know that the material standards of living, the physical satisfactions of life, are very far from the whole story. I maintain that in an industrial civilization business leaders must assume the responsibility for increasing all the human satisfactions of the group with which they are associated.[1]

[1] *Responsibilities of Business Leadership*, edited by Harwood F. Merrill (Cambridge, Harvard University Press, 1948), pp. xiv-xv.

Here is one place where it looks to me as if religion may actually have something of help to business. Or, switching the businessman's attitude which was mentioned earlier, we might find the clergyman saying: "*I* am not understood by the businessman."

At this point I was going to say that I was familiar with only one religion, Christianity. But, as I began to say it, I stopped short. For I discovered that Religion, in that sense, would have to be spelled with a capital R, and the opening position of Mr. Blank was that we were looking for something broader than that —something for which he had no word, something that was probably included in Religion, but something that did not include *all* the things which he had seen in Religion, the churches, and sectarianism.

Then I recalled that all civilizations I had read about, both primitive and highly developed, contained some notions of a god or gods, some accepted concepts of values beyond the mere material. To some scholars, at least, there is strong evidence that man is more than chemical elements. And so, inasmuch as our civilization has been deeply affected by Christianity and in many respects professes to recognize its relationship to Christianity, why not go ahead and look at this business responsibility for giving human satisfactions in the light of Christian principles, on a first assumption that Christianity and this vaguer "spiritual something" may possibly be close kin?

Could it not be possible, for instance, that the act of recognizing workers as people with hopes, ambitions, and fears, in short with human dignity as individuals, might be the same thing that Christianity calls charity? Is it not within the realm of possibility that the businessman—through the difficult task of learning the hard way, through discovering the effect on profits and losses, through essentially materialistic approaches—is "discovering" what the Church, even with a capital C, has known for centuries?

Take the problem of St. Paul. He was a preacher; that was his business. Referring to himself, he said:

Though I speak with the tongues of men and of angels, and have not charity, I am become as sounding brass, or a tinkling cymbal. And though I have the gift of prophecy, and understand all mysteries, and all knowledge; and though I have all faith, so that I could remove mountains, and have not charity, I am nothing.[2]

I do not pretend to know, but I am merely asking if there may not be a parallel between St. Paul and the businessman. He was trying to be a preacher and discovered that all the technical skills of the preacher were of no avail if he had not charity. Business executives seem also to have discovered that all the techniques of business acumen are somewhat ineffective if they overlook what sounds like a simple fact: people are individuals.

Businessmen, to be sure, now recognize that a sincere interest on their part in the worker as an individual is "good business." Everyone has heard examples which illustrate the effectiveness of the boss who knows all the men who work for him by their first names. Many also believe, however, that bosses who do things merely because they are "good human relations techniques" do not find them effective. Individuals are remarkably keen to detect insincerity, so the techniques work only when the motive behind them is sincere. Could this be what St. Paul meant when he went on to say, "Charity suffereth long and is kind; charity envieth not; charity vaunteth not itself, is not puffed up; doth not behave itself unseemly, seeketh not its own, is not easily provoked."

Religion, even organized Religion, has been dealing with individuals for centuries and in its cumulated experience probably knows quite a lot about them, both as individuals and as groups. Business, too, has been dealing with individuals for a long time, but only recently has it seemed to recognize their importance. Some observers seem to believe that our so-called "industrial civilization," by destroying many of the previous anchors of individuals, by forcing them to be parts of groups, which in many ways are significant to individual happiness, has developed new problems which the previous experience of business has not given businessmen the ability to solve. In their groping for new methods for attacking these new problems, in their acceptance of new techniques—especially in the area of psychology, for instance—have they not demonstrated their recognition of the need for skills and knowledge outside what previously had been thought of as

[2] I Corinthians 13:1-2.

the businessman's fields? I merely ask if businessmen do not owe it to themselves to see what religion or Religion has to offer them.

Concept of Humility

The second clue which I have found to the possible interrelation of business and spiritual values also comes from David's attempts to explore the meaning of the responsibilities of business—in the face of the cockiness of some businessmen who seek to be leaders. He would agree, I am sure, with the force of the question—posed by a man with a record of being a thoughtful and sympathetic observer of business—as to why businessmen are so confident that they know the answers to all the terrifying problems of making this economy of ours function, and so alarmed by everyone who criticizes anything business has done.

As desirable characteristics of the business leader, David urges first of all competence, but then humility. It is not impossible to demonstrate that religion, or some spiritual force, is one wellspring of humility. Some may deny that it is the only source; for the characteristic of intellectual honesty can also produce humility in the most competent and learned. This I accept. But, once again I merely ask, does not business owe it to itself—if it finds that humility with respect to its own ability to solve all the problems of the world is good—to investigate what religion, which has always advocated humility, has learned about the subject?

It is interesting to me that competence and humility somehow are paradoxical characteristics to find together. And yet it is not difficult to show that life itself is in many respects paradoxical—and probably religion too because it is part of life. There is a statement in connection with religion that "heresy is pushing a truth too far."

No one should be better aware than the business executive that a lot of different truths, a lot of different and contradictory facts, must be put together into a working whole. The problem of keeping balance in a complicated whole is one of the businessman's central tasks. He knows, for instance, that security is desirable but that, if it is pushed too hard, it vanishes by the very attempt to attain it. He knows, too, that change is inevitable and that to resist it completely is foolhardy, but that to move some things too fast is likewise dangerous. Possession of the skill and judgment needed to keep all facts—all truths—in balance so that results are accomplished is the businessman's real claim to responsibility. Here too, as I see it, religion comes into the picture.

Maintaining Balance

The more successful organized religions have attempted to integrate religion into the whole of a man's life, and without letting even the truth of religion be pushed too far. When religion gets pushed too far, religious fanatics or overscrupulous slaves to religion result. Educators and religious leaders alike have frequently pleaded for the development of the "whole man"; they dislike unbalanced programs which allow any aspect of a person or a society to be pushed too far.

Anyone will admit that judgment as to what is a proper balance will vary from time to time and from one person or group of persons to another. Once again, however, I am only asking if the businessman, facing a problem which has been faced by others, could not benefit from their experiences.

Religion also enters into the problem of maintaining balance for the very simple reason that religion, spiritual values, accepted codes of conduct—the phraseology makes little difference—are part of the facts of life. They are part of the whole which has to be kept in balance. It seems to me that anyone who "makes believe" such forces do not exist, or who insists they should not be as they are, or who wishes they did not exist, is closing his eyes to the real problems which he is trying to face.

I hope that this article is not interpreted as a sermon of one who is preaching. I am simply expressing here a fear that the "truths of business" may be getting pushed too far, in either or both of two ways:

(1) By overconfidence in their own ability to solve all the problems of the world, some businessmen may be undermining public confidence in their ability to solve even their own problems. Strangely enough, such lack of humility frequently results in a purely defensive and "misunderstood" attitude in the presentation of the case for the business position on national and international affairs, rather than in a constructive application of the businessman's undoubted competence to deal with certain

kinds of problems beyond the scope of his own business. By consciously or unconsciously rejecting the skills, experiences, and attitudes of other important groups, the businessman not only may be shutting himself off from useful help in his own problems, but he also may be closing the door to his own effective participation in general affairs.

(2) In espousing the responsibilities of business, especially for contributing to human happiness, I believe there is some possibility that the businessman is in danger of accepting responsibilities beyond those which are rightly his, beyond those which he can in fact fulfill, and that, without being fully aware of its implication, he is extending himself into an area where he must cooperate with others who also have responsibilities for contributing to those same human satisfactions.

I only ask that the businessman check to see if my fears have any justification and, if so, that he explore rather than ignore the part which religion might play in business and in the bigger drama of which business is but a part.

"On the Same Side"

If, then, the businessman's responsibility for contributing to human satisfactions is closely akin to what religion calls charity, and if the flavor of human relations may be improved by a dash of the Christian virtue of humility, there may be other places where business and religion could both benefit if they knew each other a little better.

For instance, one does not pursue such thoughts as these very long without coming up to the phrase "the dignity of man," because it offers perhaps the only valid reason for giving consideration to the feelings of men in dealing with them. Some may claim that the phrase is little more than a slogan exploited by organized Religion, while others may believe that religion—not the institution, but rather the concept that man is different from the other animals and therefore seems to have some moral values—has been a staunch friend of the basic tenets of private property, freedom, and democracy. It seems to me that there are many evidences and many reasons for business and religion being in fact "on the same side," and businessmen and religious men need not be mutually exclusive terms.

Rule of Action

But what is the practical value of all this? Suppose businessmen do perchance find that religion has some relationship to their problems. What do they do about it? Once again, my answer to the question must be: "I do not know." The appropriate action must be left to each businessman. The reason for this, I believe, lies in the central theme of what we are talking about: the wholeness of men whose occupational, economic, human, spiritual, religious, and other aspects are separable only in abstract thought and not in reality. The business leader, like the people whom he might lead, is a human individual. Any application of religion he makes to people must include himself and probably has to start there.

This suggests to me that maybe one rule of action is discernible: no matter what is done, the *form* of action must not be accepted as satisfactory in itself, apart from the *motive* behind what is done. For instance, one company has appointed a "vice president in charge of Christian relations." I am not saying such a move is wrong, but I am certain it would not be "right" unless it were supported by a sincere conviction that it was right. Similarly, the most successful action might not be apparent as action at all. If a businessman learned something he could use, it seems to me all that would happen is that he would begin to use it.

2.

Business Leadership and a Creative Society

BY ABRAM T. COLLIER*

High on the list of tasks facing the business administrator are those relating to the basic attitudes, interests, and objectives of his employees. Meeting antagonism and misunderstanding, as he often does, his immediate reaction is to cry out: "How can I get across to my employees some understanding of the objectives I seek?" Well, that question may be important, but perhaps it should not have such priority. It might be better to ask first: "What, in truth, do I seek? What objectives do I have that my employees can also share?"

Some administrators, of course, have not bothered their heads with such intricate problems, feeling that "only results count" or "actions speak louder than words." But advertising and public relations men have demonstrated how inadequate this view is; words and the things they connote are as much a part of our experience as the things that we perceive immediately and directly. And top-rank administrators such as Chester I. Barnard know also that one of the first and greatest functions of leadership is that the leader express for his group the ideals toward which they all, consciously or unconsciously, strive.

Winston Churchill's powerful "blood, sweat, and tears" speech

* Mr. Collier is vice president and general counsel of John Hancock Mutual Life Insurance Company.

in 1940 has now become a classic model in the political field of the way in which a leader can express the purpose of the people and rally them to common effort. Businessmen, especially those of us concerned with personnel, productivity, and morale, have come to recognize the need for much the same kind of leadership, convinced that only in this way will employees ever have the satisfaction of really feeling they are identified with the enterprise for which they work.

But in seeking to exert such leadership we have already learned that there are some difficult problems of communication in the way. Take the many attempts that have been made in recent years, following the example of such companies as Du Pont, General Electric, and Republic Steel, to give supervisors and workers in business some understanding of the economic and political society in which we live. The general experience is that the terms "capitalism," "competition," "American way of life," "land of opportunity," and "free private enterprise," through excessive repetition, abuse, or otherwise, have lost much of their capacity to convey the meaning intended.

Moreover, where new symbols have been introduced for the old, they too have missed the mark. The editors of *Fortune*, for example, have characterized our society as the "permanent revolution," but we do not think of ourselves as revolutionaries—at least not of the black-bearded and bomb-carrying kind. Other attempts to call our society "open" or "free" have raised the perplexing questions: Open for what? Free for what?

It seems to me that we businessmen ought to aim at articulating an ideology that, in addition to being an accurate expression of management goals, is a little closer to the personal and even religious aspirations of the people than anything we have espoused in the past. Is it not possible that we have been thinking too much in terms of systems, of economics, of products, of laws? Perhaps these approaches should not have failed as they did; perhaps they can be improved. But in any event it seems to me that the fact of their failure (or, at best, their lack of any great success) should be accepted, and that the most profitable line of inquiry is to turn to a different sort of approach altogether.

The Creative Ideal

Accordingly, I put forward this simple proposition: that our society is a creative society; that its prime objective, as well as its great genius, is its creativeness; and that, as creative accomplishment is the actual day-to-day goal of modern business, it is also the keystone of our business philosophy.

I am thinking of creativeness in its widest and deepest sense. Thus, business does not exist merely to produce more goods and services, or better goods and services for more people, though that is no small part of its task. Business also, particularly in these days, affords the principal or the only means whereby individual men may gain the satisfaction of accomplishing something more than merely sustaining their own lives. Pleasure, power, and fame appear to be but by-products of the efforts we make to be useful members of society and to leave it with something more than it had when we arrived. Perhaps we leave only the grain of sand that Robert Frost said he wished to leave on the beach of history; but at least, if we do that, we can feel that we have fulfilled our role in living.

What I am suggesting is that the great goals of happiness, freedom, security—even goodness and truth—are values which should be viewed as subordinate to, and resulting from, a new and positive creative ideal. Our people in business and elsewhere seem to be driven by an urge to build; by a longing to explore and reach out; by a desire to realize, through men and for men, such things and experiences as humanity has never known before. In this light, our vaunted freedoms of thought and action, our sought-for freedoms from worry and want, and even our ethical standards of behavior (products as they are of other places and times) are not ends in themselves; rather they emerge as important values just because they support and make possible a creative society of men.

This is the modern heresy: that it is not enough to be good, to lead a blameless life; we must also be creative.

The New and the Old

In one sense this ideal is modern in expression only. Wise men in almost every age have been trying to tell us that the greatest individual satisfaction there is comes from a job well done. Samuel Johnson, for example, observed: "Life affords no higher pleasure than that of surmounting difficulties, passing from one step of success to another, forming new wishes and seeing them gratified." And Emerson said: "The *sum* of wisdom is that the time is never lost that is devoted to work."

In another sense, however, this ideal of ours shows some new, significantly new, aspects. Specifically, in American business it is now beginning to be recognized that *everyone* has the capacity for the satisfaction that comes from creative accomplishment. As science unleashes vast new sources of power, it appears possible for the first time in history for men of all types and classes to avoid the toil and suffering of hard labor and to experience the joys of work—a satisfaction which in times past was limited to the few.

Contrast this with the older view. We used to classify as creative only those accomplishments that certain individuals could achieve. The writer, the artist, the composer, the scientist—in other words, the rare people who had the genius to find and express new ideas or new truths—were considered the creative members of our society; the classic examples have been the Newtons, the Beethovens, the Kants, the Michelangelos, the Shakespeares. The magnitude of their work often crushed us by making us feel our own inadequacy.

Today, however, we are beginning to recognize that creative work may be accomplished collectively as well as individually. The great and small organizations that have built and operated our industrial plants, farms, transportation and communication networks, financial systems, and distributive organizations, all are examples of the creative genius which comes from the collective effort of administrators and workers, as well as specialists of all degrees.

Dimension of the Task

The first task of business leaders, therefore, is to create an environment in which there can flourish not only individual genius but, more important, the collective capacities of other people in the organization. Some difficult and searching questions must be answered if this task is to be accomplished. What are the basic positive forces operating in a creative business society? What generates their power? What keeps them in balance? What conditions their survival? What controls their direction?

To this end, I should like to submit that the creative ideal depends on the following concepts:

(1) That the forces in business (and many other types of organization) are nurtured by the existence of *differences between individuals and groups.*

(2) That these forces are kept in control and balance by the process of *individuals understanding each other.*

(3) That a creative society depends for its survival on the belief that *rights must be matched by obligations.*

(4) That the directing force in a creative society is the *faith* of its members in *individual growth.*

THE POWER OF DIFFERENCE

In considering the importance of individual differences, it should first be noted that the goal of many societies—including the goal of Communist society today and of almost every Utopia that has ever been conceived, from Plato to Aldous Huxley—has been to compel men to conform. The theory is that if everyone is induced to accept the same ideas of what is good and proper, conflicts between men and groups of men will disappear and humanity will live happily ever after.

By contrast, one of the cornerstones on which the creative society is built is the incontrovertible fact that men are different, that they cherish these differences, that the joy and fascination of life depends on the existence of differences, and that there are great social values in differences.

Driving Force

Every great ideal has its own theory of the nature of man. The wholly competitive or acquisitive society, which is gone (if it ever in fact existed), assumed that man was motivated only by his own pleasure, that he was egoistic and greedy, and that his wants were insatiable. By assuming that the average man, the economic man, was moved by animal impulses, it was possible to work out satisfactory theoretical explanations of how men acted in the market place.

On the other hand, socialists have assumed, following the notions of Rousseau (and possibly the story of Genesis), that man was essentially good, self-sacrificing, considerate, and loving, but was corrupted by social institutions. On this basis they thought that if institutions were changed or destroyed and if nonconforming individuals and classes were eliminated, then all social problems would cease and the state could and would wither away.

But in a creative society neither of these views is adequate. We observe that men are both egoistic and self-sacrificing—and many things more. While men are, taken as a whole, driven by an urge to create and grow, their characteristics vary with their times, experiences, culture, inheritance, and with all the other circumstances in which they find themselves. To illustrate with a simple example:

In the company with which I am associated we are using, as an aid in selection and placement, a test of personality or temperament in which the results are described not in imprecise words but in graphic form. Taking several major behavior characteristics, it plots with a fair degree of accuracy where a given individual falls on each of several temperament spectra. For instance, there is a spectrum of gregariousness in which the extreme extrovert falls at one end and the extreme introvert at the other; in between are those having various needs for sociability or a capacity to live within themselves.

Thousands upon thousands of tests of this type have been made, and it is fair to say that in no two cases have the results—the combinations of characteristics on the several spectra—been exactly the same. Similarity of types may be observed, but every man and every woman is found to be unique. Furthermore, research into personality shows that men change their personalities, usually extremely slowly but sometimes dramatically. It also shows that behavior is not wholly a matter for the individual alone but depends in large part on the situation in which he finds himself. That is, the set of values according to which he makes his decisions may vary with his external circumstances.

The driving force of difference—in individuals and in groups—seems well illustrated by the history of the United States and Canada (in contrast to some other countries). While no doubt we have strong forces in many companies, labor unions, churches, and schools which are trying to enforce a high degree of conformity to some particular viewpoint, practice, or belief, nevertheless those forces have been observably less dominant than the forces of individual integrity. In our business world, if a man has felt that he could do a job better than someone else, he has been free to try; indeed, the fact that he saw things differently has given him both the opportunity and the courage to try.

Moreover, there is good reason to believe that the differences between groups of people in the United States and Canada with respect to cultural, racial, and religious backgrounds have been a factor in the dynamic development of these countries. What does it mean that never before in history have so many diverse religious groups been able to live together with so little disharmony? Has our society progressed *in spite of* differences or *because of* them? Possibly the very existence of differences among various people and groups has given people the courage to disagree with prevailing opinions. Every discovery, every invention, every new industry, every new idea has come about because some person or some group of people has had the courage as well as the insight to disagree with the majority or do what the majority has not thought of doing before. This is perhaps part of what David McCord Wright had in mind when he pointed out:

> Our dilemma . . . is that if we make men "free," they will become creative and from their creations will spring the probability of growth and the certainty of trouble.[1]

Diversity Rather than Conflict

Differences do, of course, lead to trouble—to misunderstanding and conflict. Yet conflict is essential to constructive work. More than a generation ago Mary Parker Follett, recognized for her many profound insights into the nature of business organizations, wrote:

> What people often mean by getting rid of conflict is getting rid of diversity, and it is of the utmost importance that these should not be con-

[1] *The Impact of the Union* (New York, Harcourt, Brace and Company, Inc., 1951), p. 274.

sidered the same. We may wish to abolish conflict, but we cannot get rid of diversity. We must face life as it is and understand that diversity is its most essential feature. . . . Fear of difference is dread of life itself. It is possible to conceive conflict as not necessarily a wasteful outbreak of incompatibilities but a *normal* process by which socially valuable differences register themselves for the enrichment of all concerned.[2]

Creativeness in an organization depends to a large extent on people who are not too ready to agree. In our own experience, most of us abhor the attitude of "Well, if you're going to argue about it, let's do it your way." We have found that we must have diversity of opinion, firmly as well as fairly expressed, if our business is to make the wise decisions that will enable it to develop and grow.

If we accept difference, it necessarily follows that we are not sure we are right ourselves; we accept the notion that our conclusions about people and society must be treated only as working hypotheses and that there are realities beyond those of our immediate perceptions. It is sometimes forgotten how highly we esteem this concept in the physical sciences. The entire atomic world of neutrons and electrons has never been perceived directly; despite Hiroshima and Nagasaki, it is still a theory or a working hypothesis. The same hypothetical character pertains to all of our knowledge about genes—the transmission of traits from organisms to their offspring.

But if it is necessary to trust to more than our immediate perceptions in the physical sciences, it would seem even more important to do so in social, ethical, and political matters that deal with human beings. The observation of Yale's F. C. S. Northrop, that the ability to live in a world of both immediate perceptions and unperceived hypotheses is the essence of the genius of the West, would apply no less to our industrial and political society than to our scientific progress.

This means that we must subject our old concepts of right and wrong, of good and bad, to a radical change; things are no longer so black and white. Judge Learned Hand, philosopher as well as judge, has described the spirit of liberty as "the spirit that is not too sure that it is right." Tolerance for difference, for the view-

2 *Creative Experiences* (New York, Longmans, Green & Co., 1924), pp. 300, 301.

point that we do not agree with, implies that we are not so sure of our own. We accept our principles of action as working hypotheses, realizing that something may happen to lead us to revise these opinions. While it often sounds as though some of our friends would never change their opinions (particularly on matters of ethics or politics), our great genius lies in the fact that we may talk loudly but, when the chips are down, we seem to act on the basis that all general rules of what is right and wrong must be tempered by common sense.

It can be reasonably contended that the great upheavals of modern history—its wars and its revolutions—are not so much the result of differences between people as of the feeling of a nation or a class that its capacity for creative expression is in some way threatened or thwarted. This was one cause of the Russian revolt of 1917, although the revolutionaries themselves later made the great and historic blunder of seeking to abolish conflict by abolishing difference rather than by accepting difference and in that way removing the barriers to creative work.

Nations such as ours, that have insisted on the freedom of their people to be different, have had to fight and may well fight again to preserve their right to disagree with one another. Yet, if the principle of difference is one of the cornerstones of creativeness, our society has little to fear *in the long run* from the Stalins who deny the privilege of difference to their own people.

Process of Understanding

If diversity is the first condition of the creative society, then understanding is the second. The Bible's exhortation, "with all thy getting, get understanding," is appropriate for modern industry. If for their dynamic creative power our businesses depend on continuing differences in viewpoint, for balance and braking power they must equally depend on understanding, on the felt necessity for securing agreement and cooperation.

In the sense that I am using the term, understanding refers both to self-understanding and understanding of others. Self-awareness as a desirable personal attribute is certainly not newer than the Socratic injunction, "Know thyself"; but what is new in our time is the fact that thoughtful social scientists and hardheaded businessmen are coming to see that self-awareness or self-understanding is directly related to an individual's capacity to do creative work with other people. Businessmen are beginning to think not only of the logics of business but also of what Pareto described as the nonlogics or the sentiments of people. They are beginning to see that their own behavior is a factor which influences the behavior of others, and that they are personally involved in more roles than one in every situation in which they play a part.

Let me illustrate from my own personal experience:

For a short time, some years ago, I engaged in the general practice of law. Later I became employed as a lawyer by an insurance company. As a lawyer my clients' problems were not mine; and no matter how hard I tried to solve them, I stood outside of the situation and was not involved in it. But when later I took an administrative position, I found that this detachment was no longer possible, even if I wanted it. I was personally involved in every important decision, and my behavior was affecting others. The shock of being forced to examine my own behavior was by no means small. What I needed to do, however, was no less than what all successful administrators are doing daily in every business.

In addition to self-awareness there is the need for understanding others. What we are learning today is not just that it is a "good thing to see the other fellow's point of view," but also what it is that often makes it difficult to do so. We are learning that we cannot really understand another if we agree with him, nor can we understand him if we disagree! When we feel either love or hate, we lose our power to see the world as others see it. We blur our own perceptions, and we cut off the normal flow of words which help us to see into another's mind.

Gateways to Communication

This conclusion has tremendous significance. If understanding the needs and desires of others is an essential for collective creative effort, it means that we can no longer be quick to evaluate people or their opinions as either good or bad. During the understanding process at least, we must throw our ethical judgments out the window.

Carl R. Rogers and F. J. Roethlisberger made this same point when, in essence, they said that the great barrier to communication is our tendency to evaluate, to approve or disapprove the statements that other people make.[3] For example:

If you say to me, "I prefer Englishmen to the French," there is almost an overwhelming urge for me to say either "So do I" or "No, I think they are stuffy." We may then talk for hours without a meeting of the minds. If, on the other hand, I want to find out whether we really agree or disagree about this matter, if I want to listen intelligently and to understand what you mean, thus opening the gateway to communication, then I must restrain my natural inclination to presume what you mean and instead make an effort to draw you out. I might ask something like, "Do you mean Englishmen are more to be admired?" You may reply, "Yes, they are really facing up to their economic problems better than the French." And if I continue in that way, rephrasing your comments in question form to test out what you are *trying* to tell me, there is a much better chance that we can have a fruitful discussion.

This brief explanation of a gateway to understanding, to receiving communications, to listening, may sound extremely obvious and somewhat simple. We spend most of our time learning to express ourselves, which is difficult enough but still easier than listening. Indeed, it is fair to say that listening is one of the most difficult things in the world to do. When someone charges into your office and criticizes some action that you have taken, it is not easy to find out what is really on his mind when your first impulse is to tell him to "go to hell." Or take the case where somebody asks you for your advice because he cannot make up his mind about a personal problem; most of us are inclined to comply with such a request without knowing what the real problem is, or without realizing that the decision will be sound only if it is made by the troubled person himself.

It takes real insight to be able to express in words what someone else is trying to tell us. It also takes great effort and even courage. If we put ourselves in someone else's position, if we try to express adequately his point of view, we may find that our own views become changed in the process. As Rogers says, "The risk of being

[3] "Barriers and Gateways to Communication," *Harvard Business Review*, July-August 1952, p. 46.

changed is one of the most frightening prospects many of us can face."[4]

There are, of course, many other ways of securing understanding; some of them have been outlined by Stuart Chase in his popularization of social science, *Roads to Agreement*. One is particularly worth mentioning:

This way is modeled on the long-established custom of the Quaker business meeting. Quakers as a class are great individualists, but in handling the business affairs of their churches they act only with unanimity. They have no formal voting, no sense of a majority imposing its will on a reluctant minority. If a problem cannot be settled by unanimous agreement, they invoke periods of silence or put over the question until some future meeting. Some solution is usually forthcoming.

This rule of unanimity, it seems, is now being practiced by boards of directors and executive committees in businesses throughout the land. What a far cry this is from deciding what is the greatest good for the greatest number by a mechanical counting of hands! Where difference is accepted, it is possible also to accept the notion that a minority may be right.[5]

Integration vs. Compromise

The concept of integration as opposed to compromise is also achieving a wider recognition. Integration may be called the means of solving a conflict of opinion in such a way that both sides prevail. The idea behind it is that the basic interests underlying many disputes are not inconsistent. For example:

If two people in an office want to use the same desk, it may appear at first that a major conflict is in the making, which can be solved only if one or the other wins the decision. On investigation, however, it may appear that one of the persons wants the desk in order to have better light, whereas the other wants it in order to be near some friend. If these facts come out, it will be apparent that neither wants the desk as such and that it may well be possible to satisfy the basic interests of both.

In order to achieve integrations, says Mary Parker Follett, we should "never, if possible, allow an either/or situation to be created. . . . There are almost always more than two alternatives

[4] *Ibid.*, p. 48.
[5] New York, Harper & Brothers, 1951, pp. 45 ff.

in a situation and our job is to analyze the situation carefully enough for as many as possible to appear. A yes-or-no question is in itself a prejudgment."[6]

May there not be some relationship between these methods of reaching understanding and the spirit which is not too sure that it is right? Is there not some connection between these techniques of agreement and our capacity for collective creativeness? Can it not be said that in a creative society we must have both conflict and agreement?

RIGHTS AND OBLIGATIONS

A third standard of a creative society, and an essential ingredient in our workaday world, has been foreshadowed by our discussion of difference and of understanding. It is the belief that human relationships are two-way matters and that rights are matched by obligations.

The "Double Plus"

Karl Marx predicted that in Western society it was inevitable that the rich would become richer and the poor would become poorer. This increasing division between the classes would, as he saw it, accelerate class warfare and the revolution. If our society had indeed been basically competitive and acquisitive, instead of creative and cooperative, Marx may well have been proved right. But the fact is that today, through our collective creativeness, the poor have become richer. Our society has been able to create wealth at a vastly greater rate than it has increased its population.

By and large, we have been able to maintain the viewpoint that our economic and political problem is not so much to redistribute the wealth that exists as to create more wealth for all. As the eminent economist, Kenneth E. Boulding, says, "Economic life is not a 'zero sum' poker game in which a fixed volume of wealth is circulated around among the players, but a 'positive sum' enterprise in which the accumulation of each person represents something which he brings to the 'pot' rather than something which he takes out."[7] In other words, we are engaged in a creative

[6] *Dynamic Administration—The Collected Papers of Mary Parker Follett* (New York, Harper & Brothers, 1940), pp. 219, 220.

[7] "Religious Foundations of Economic Progress," *Harvard Business Review*, May-June 1952, p. 36; also p. 126 of this volume.

task of producing more and better things. We recognize that we share as we contribute, that no society can long give something for nothing (to the poor *or* the rich), and that we cannot do great work unless *everyone* shares both in the work and in its results.

This concept has been called by many names. Mutuality is one; give-and-take is another. Professor Charles I. Gragg of the Harvard Business School called it the "double plus." In his view, business transactions and other relationships can be described in one of three ways:

(1) There is first the kind of a transaction in which the plus is all on my side, leaving a big minus for you. If I take all the profit, however, through my power or my cleverness, then I have really lost the bargain, because you will come to distrust me and will refuse to do business with me for long.

(2) The reverse situation is equally disastrous. If I, through an excess of altruism or with misguided notions of humanity, permit you to take the entire profit, with nothing for myself, I put you in the unhappy role of being a recipient of my charity; moreover, I leave myself unable to do further business with anyone.

(3) But there is still another and more satisfactory form. Only if you profit moderately and I profit moderately, only if there is a plus for you and a plus for me—a double plus—can we continue to deal with one another steadily and with confidence.

In our business lives we are beginning to see that by consciously fashioning our relationships with our employees, with our suppliers, with our customers—and, indeed, even with our competitors—we are not making suspicious and careful deals so much as common-sense arrangements that are carried on in this spirit of mutual give-and-take. That does not mean anything petty like back-scratching; every service and every kindness is not to be immediately returned, nor is every service to be performed in the hope of return. The correct attitude, rather, is a healthy respect for the well-being and personal integrity of the other fellow.

Profit to All Parties

What does all this imply? Only in an atmosphere of profit (in the broad sense) to all parties can we meet the creative objectives that our society sets. If, in times past, we erred on the side of taking too much for ourselves, it is equally essential that we do not err in the future on the side of trying to do too much for others. A too-literal application of the Sermon on the Mount—the turn of the cheek—does small damage to us but great damage to him who strikes the blow.

Why is it, otherwise, that the problem of providing for the aged worker has once more raised its head, when we thought a few years ago that we had safely tucked it away with compulsory retirement and pensioning at age sixty-five? From the point of view of sympathy for the aged and of convenience in administering our business enterprises, the practice is as desirable today as it was fifteen years ago. We have discovered, however, that many individual men who retire are hurt because they lose their sense of being creative, of being useful members of society. Moreover, when we contemplate that 11 per cent of our population will be over sixty-five in another twenty years, we begin to realize that the real economic cost of compulsory retirement is not the money that goes into pensions but the lost productivity of these older people.

It seems that people, individually and in groups, must continue to be creative; if they are not, the individual or society, or both, will suffer. If we do not intend to keep people over sixty-five in business, some other way must be found to permit them to continue active membership in the world's work.

The same kind of thinking underlies our concern for other noncontributors to society. Society has been doing an increasingly successful job of minimizing sickness of almost all kinds, not so much out of solicitude for the feelings of persons who are ill as out of its own self-interest in having the benefit of their contribution. Programs undertaken with this motive quickly earn common respect, for the galling part of illness to the sufferer is the necessity of having to depend on others, of not being able to contribute his share.

We are concerned for similar reasons about the criminal and the indolent. It is true that we have not as yet learned enough to be confident of our ability to rehabilitate these people. But we have at least learned that it is no answer to judge them or to punish them; our first task is to understand them. We consider them "cured" only when they join the majority of their fellows, contributing commensurately to what they receive.

Why do businessmen fight against the welfare state? Are businessmen actually heartless and callous? Don't they recognize that the sick and the poor need the aid of the rest who are well and able? Of course they do. But their experience says to them that doctors do not give pills to everyone because a few are sick; that when a man is given something for which he has not worked, he feels degraded; that a man who is well and able wants to earn what he receives.

Businessmen, who have learned from experience that paternalism has failed, hope that government will learn from their mistakes. Businessmen have good reason for believing that government will not really serve the poor and sick until it stops regarding them as "little people," and undertakes instead the harder job of giving them an honest chance to do useful and creative work.

FAITH IN MEN'S GROWTH

The fourth and last condition of maintaining and strengthening a creative society, the force that provides direction and control, is a clear faith in the growth and development of men. The machine age poses a great challenge to our willingness to demonstrate this faith. All of the new wealth we can produce with modern technology is of little avail if in the process men are reduced to the levels of the machines they tend. But fortunately we are not confronted with a Hobson's choice between wealth and men. We have found that the more we are able to train and develop men as individuals, leaving repetitive work to machines, the greater satisfactions they obtain and the more productive (in a material sense) they become.

Take a business with a large content of routine clerical work, e.g., life insurance. In this business we stand on the threshold of a new era in adapting electronics to office workers' problems. When any business reaches this point, to be sure, management is bound to face the problem of securing the cooperation of people who may prefer things as they are. It may even have to face a problem of technological unemployment. But however real and thorny these difficulties are, they are insignificant compared to the human values that are gained. Instead of a business in which, say, 75 per cent of the employees are engaged in routine tasks, the modern machine makes it possible for 75 per cent to be engaged in tasks requiring skill and judgment. The machine eliminates human toil; but, much more important, it also provides opportunities for men to do only those tasks men alone can do.

New Concept of Organization

The development of the machine economy has numerous important implications for management. For one thing, it is fast bringing about a new concept of business organization. No longer can the boss know all the details and the intricacies of the operation he supervises. He is being forced more and more to rely on his subordinates, to consult with them, to be guided by their joint conclusions—in short, to permit them to share and to grow in breadth of vision.

This in turn means, of course, a gradual abandonment of authoritarian principles. Administrators have begun to conceive of their role not as manipulators of labor but as coordinators of functions. Re-examining themselves and their jobs, they have discovered that they have no special claim to superior wisdom, no vested authority over the work and lives of others. They have found, rather, that they have a function to perform: to plan ahead, to coordinate the others, to secure their interest and cooperation.

Society will not, as a result, tend to become classless in any Marxian sense. Far from it. We may reasonably anticipate, however, that members of future "elites" will come to occupy positions of status and power less because of wealth, position, or birth and more because of the kind of contributions they make or because of the kind of functions they fulfill. Key positions will tend more and more to be occupied by those who are best able to conceive new ideas and the application of old ones, who are best able to communicate ideas and events, and who are best able to pull together people and things to achieve creative ends. Today's inheritance tax and management's increased interest in personnel development are fast speeding this process along.

Administrators as Teachers

In an important sense the role of the administrator seems destined to become more and more that of the instructor—the kind of teacher who understands his pupils, accepts their differences, commands their respect, and inspires them to creative work of every kind. In such a role, administrators will have less of a problem of discipline to the degree that they are able to develop an environment for creative experience and to lead their students (their workers) to savor the satisfying taste of personal accomplishment. In so doing they will have gone far to eliminate the distinction between "schooling" and "education" which Mark Twain properly made when he quipped, "I have never let my schooling interfere with my education."

In their new role as teachers, administrators are learning that attitudes and viewpoints which affect behavior can frequently be communicated effectively only if they are reduced to concrete terms. In their efforts at training and development, particularly, they are recognizing the need to start from real case situations. Witness the growing attention to discussions of actual business problems rather than the oft-repeated clichés on general principles of management.

Abstract ideas, however, are not to be discarded simply because they so often fail to influence behavior. Indeed, as the mark of civilized men they are necessary tools of communication which are quite adequate *if* both writer and reader start from the same premises. They are easily accepted, in other words, if they seem meaningful in relation to one's own experience. Aneurin Bevan's autobiography affords an example of this:

Bevan's life as a young Welsh miner was filled with frustrations. Then he read Karl Marx. This experience "had all the impact of divine revelation. Everything fell in place. The dark places were lighted up and the difficult ways made easy."[8] Marx is most abstract, but nevertheless his words have had a great effect on people whose experience has led them to feel like chained and exploited men.

The moral of this fact has not been lost on businessmen and statesmen, who know that the only real and lasting bulwark against Marxism is in the experience of the large body of our workers and our citizens. If that experience is basically creative and satisfying—and it is management's task to see that it is so—the stultifying conformities of the socialist state will always be bitter to their taste.

[8] *In Place of Fear* (New York, Simon and Schuster, Inc., 1952), p. 19.

But businessmen and statesmen, while often seeing what is the best *defense* against Marxism, have not been so quick to see what needs to be done in a *positive* way. Like Marxians, we too must have an appropriate body of abstract ideas—ideas that can constitute a simple article of faith but are also capable of profound extension, ideas that are consistent with experience but are also adaptable to new insights and new truths.

Perhaps this discussion will stimulate others to work out such ideas—each in his own way, as a part of our individual differences, but all toward the same goal, in the spirit of mutuality. What I have written can be no more than a preface.

Conclusion

The problems of production, distribution, and finance are usually foreign to a worker's experience and interests. It is therefore just as silly for top management to hope that workers will be anxious to understand the problems of the business as it would be to fear that they are interested in gaining control of the business. What workers do appear to want is a chance to increase their usefulness and creativeness, a chance to develop their full potential as individuals within the scope of their environment and experience. It has become part of management's function to see not only that they have that chance but that the philosophy behind it is made articulate.

But the creative society is based on more than the relationship between management and workers, indispensable though that is in our industrial age. It depends on close relationships between all fields of human endeavor. Business is not "just business." The Chinese wall between business and the home, the community, the school, and the church has long since been stormed. Business is all people, places, and things; it is physics, economics, politics, sociology, psychology, philosophy, ethics, and aesthetics.

In the same broad sense, business is also religion. One of the recurring themes in most religions is that God is viewed as the Creator and that creativeness is one of His essential attributes. Another recurring theme is that man's spirit, his conscious "self," his unique ability to transcend his material and animal limitations, is the essence of God in man. To suggest that creativeness may be a basic attribute of men in society is thus merely to relate these two age-less insights.

Moreover, a religious sense of wonder, humility, and faith helps us to see the vision of a boundless future built by the inherent capacities of men from all walks of life and of all races, creeds, natures, and backgrounds. It is a vision of cooperation, together-ness, and sharing the great adventure. It is a vision of independence and courage that explores the far reaches of the universe and probes deep into the essence of what we call man. It is, in short, a vision of a changing, growing, and infinitely exciting world which depends for its existence on the spirit that is not too sure it is right, on a deep-seated desire to open our minds and our hearts to the lives of others, on the practical sense of give-and-take, on our faith in the growth and development of ourselves and our fellow men.

3.

The Mainspring of Business Leadership

By Paul Cifrino*

In a sense it is a discouraging task to write about the problems of leadership and employer morale. The wisdom of the ages contains, I believe, all that is worth knowing about them. The best any writer can do, therefore, is to restate the old insights in contemporary terms, drawing on personal observation and the wealth of illustrative material in industrial relations research. But, within these limits, I think that there are some important things that need to be said about the job of the business leader today.

Most of us would agree that American workers are on the whole well managed. The question is whether this is so because of the contemporary approach to leadership and personnel management or in spite of it. Our time, like any other time in history, has its blind spots—caused, as so often happens, by infatuation with those techniques at which we think we excel. I am thinking in particular of certain ideas that are much in vogue about the art of leadership, human relations, industrial relations, and so on.

Because of these blind spots business leaders today tend to overlook a number of crucial propositions, and it is these that I want to discuss in the following pages:

Contrary to what so much of the prevailing theory about leadership and employee relations implies (without actually coming out and saying

* Mr. Cifrino is general manager of Supreme Markets, a supermarket food chain in metropolitan Boston.

32

it), workers *do* like to work and do *not* need to be "sold" on the value of doing a good job or "motivated" into action. The company environment itself is capable of arousing strong interest and loyalty on the part of employees.

We need to take more of a nonemotional, nonpersonal approach to loyalty, leadership, and participation. The emotional, the intuitive, the nonscientific factors that draw men together are fundamental; but any attempt to control them develops an artificiality and is likely to boomerang. The native, basic, emotional drives of human nature to belong and to cooperate should be permitted to develop freely and impulsively, without any tampering. Management need only provide a decent company environment among normal, decent people.

Leadership is the representation of the company (or a department or work level) by an individual person. It is weakened, however, by public relations build-ups and other manipulative practices which, although designed to strengthen leadership, misfire because of the faulty assumptions on which they are based.

Our emphasis on surface techniques of manipulation is unworthy and unwise. Productivity is related not to happiness but to morality—the morality of high standards. There is a good deal of truth still in the old insight that "people like a tough boss." Workers' responses and loyalties range in every direction; there is no one pattern which correlates in any sensible fashion with performance on the job.

Creativity and Cooperation

Let us begin with the assumption that a person is a being created and possessed by that mysterious "Principle of Organization" which so many scientists and philosophers have been searching for through time and space. Whatever is the primal force that makes atoms and molecules and cells and living things revolve and flow, combine and grow, strive blindly and seek consciously toward ever larger and more complex patterns of individuality and organization—this force reveals itself also in man.

The simple fact is that men work and build because it is part of their nature—possibly the largest part—to do so. Only in terms so fundamental can we explain why men so often do creative things without any motive of self-interest. Only in terms so universal can we comprehend the cooperative actions of so many different kinds of men in such diverse conditions of time, place, and environment.

Here is a healthy beginning for understanding and practicing leadership: this reverent belief that the creative spirit exists in all men. It follows that if all men do not show it to the same degree, there is nothing we can do as leaders to call it into being for them; we can only provide a climate in which it will have greater scope to express itself.

Work Community—Utopia

Man has always sought to live in a harmonious and ordered world—this being the ultimate efficient form of creative organization. And when the real world has proved too unmalleable, men have explored for or invented philosophic "kingdoms of perfection."

Consider, for example, the passionate interest in sports, even on the part of people who have never, or only barely, participated. There are many causes, but surely part of the great appeal of sports is that the rules are the same for everybody and are invariably upheld, that dishonesty is never countenanced, that the team members are always loyal and (on the surface at least) always give their best, that the judges are impartial, and that the best man usually wins. This "wonderful world of sports" presents in miniature a variety of utopias embodying justice, logic, order, and balance. There are surprises, but they are based on performance or fortune and not on human caprice.

Does not business offer a parallel? A worker may feel that the work environment leaves something to be desired. But it does possess to a very real degree some of the same attractions as the world of sports. It tends to be more stable and orderly than the larger world with all of its anomalies, contradictions, and cruelties. Most of the deeper passions and emotional impulses which trouble the tide of affairs are removed from the industrial world—not completely, of course, but enough to make work a different kind of existence.

So the work community, to the extent that it is in fact well ordered and integrated, can arouse a deep loyalty—and not because of the virtues or personalities of the managers, but because all people are Don Quixotes searching for justice or, in modern terms, seeking to engage themselves in cooperative activity toward accepted goals, a uniform discipline, and a familiar set of techniques. Progress can be felt—not without the usual growth pains, of course, but at least growth is orderly. The criteria for judging performance and allocating rewards are relatively objective and, far more than contemporary folklore would have it, reasonably inde‧pendent of whim or nepotism. All of this stems from and appeals to that great basic drive toward expression and organization exist‧ing in all men.

Management—End in Itself

We often hear it said today that the only major goal of a busi‧ness is to create and expand markets. But a business, being mind‧less, is without goals; the goals must be in the minds of people— the owners or, in today's economy, the managers. And since people are complex human beings, they have many motivations. While it might be tidier if business managers had as their major and only direct goal the creation of customers, in this real world these real men will be driven by more than commercial dynamics. Managers have a deep urge to mold and control the internal environment created by their industrial activity. They are passionately involved in this environment *for its own sake*—and not simply because it is also a means to a commercial end.

These facts make the manager different from the professional or technical man. The professional deals mainly with nonrecurring or unconnected individual cases—clients, patients, students, and so forth; the technician deals mainly with the application of a specific body of theoretical knowledge. When the firm of the professional or technician grows large and he spends most of his time adjusting per‧sonalities and work situations, he becomes in fact a manager. This happens to a physician when he passes from medical practice to hos‧pital administration, or to a teacher when he becomes a dean, or to a scientist when he goes from the laboratory to research manage‧ment.

In addition, then, to his traditional economic role, the business manager creates or maintains environments which other people will share. Also, from this smaller, more limited, and more per‧fectible industrial community he—like every other participant— may derive knowledge of value to him as a citizen in the larger world. This fact has many social implications, yet it has received scant attention from our novelists and playwrights. It is time that business managers ceased to be the perpetually underprivileged of literature.[1]

But when the manager's environment-shaping activity is discussed, it is usually considered an instrument, a tool, or a technique. We tend to say, in effect: "Of course the manager will seek to achieve this fine result because a stable work situation controls costs, increases sales, or develops bright young men for expansion."

Such a statement overlooks a very important aspect of leadership. When a manager seeks to develop and participate in a rational, orderly work system, do not his efforts reflect the innate, basic, primal drive toward organization which is possessed by him and the workers he manages? If that is so, management is not just a means, but an *end in itself*.

This Business of "Belonging"

Many of our business thinkers have recently made the "discovery" that there is a drive to "belong" and have suggested ways to exploit it. Their phraseology itself implies a certain artificiality since they speak of a "sense" or "feeling" of belonging as if it were something more imagined than real. Now, men have known, since they began to think, that living beings are subject to a vital force drawing them toward one another. This urge, which is reflected in the emotional and intuitive side of human nature, is wholly different from the creative personality forces just discussed. Every poet and prophet has felt it; indeed, it is the guiding principle of oriental religious thought. There are great satisfactions which spring from submergence of individual identity in a shared activity —satisfactions not always pretty or controllable, as witness the solidarity of a lynching mob.

In the light of this, do appeals directed to the emotional and sentimental part of human nature represent a proper management activity? The web which binds man to man is too broad, too tangled, and too pervasive; the actions which spring from these relationships are too unpredictable. That is why any surface manipulation is likely to boomerang.

[1] See Kenneth S. Lynn, "Authors in Search of the Businessman," *Harvard Business Review*, September-October 1956, p. 116.

It is easy to arouse emotional feelings of group belonging. This is done all the time at employee socials, at Christmas parties, and so on. Unfortunately, the feelings vanish as quickly as they come. Here is no foundation for erecting an organization, but only an emotional quicksand. There is no way of confining these emotional tendencies to a particular work group or purpose. The worker who is most carried away by the old "company spirit" is probably just as susceptible to feelings of union brotherhood.

MORALE AND LOYALTY

It seems not only safer but more constructive to relate the job of the business leader to the other, more logical side of human nature—where the need to belong to an organization is a directable, purposeful, *intellectual* force. Here we shall be considering not "rhythms of the heart" but "rhythms of the head."

Let us think of this intellectual kind of belonging as the sharing of constructive activity, and let us call it *involvement*. Participation is another term, but it carries certain emotional overtones that are best avoided. The objective is very simple and straightforward: to involve the worker in the *work* situation. That—nothing less and nothing more—is what he is there for, and that is what we want him for.

Why should we care whether workers identify themselves with the bowling team, the twenty-year club, or the "big, happy family" —sentimental activities which, properly conducted, may do them no harm and may even give some superficial enjoyment, but which are not really related to their work at all?

As matter of fact, if the work situation does not influence the employee's family or social life, I think that is a healthy sign; the involvement does not carry over because it is nonemotional. Among the best workers there are many who bring little or nothing of their work home with them. Before we consider this a failing, let us recall that some of the great captains of history had the ability to shut up a section of the mind—as one would close a drawer, to use Napoleon's analogy—and then to turn lightheartedly to recreation.

Involvement is essential to morale and peak performance; it also satisfies one of man's basic personal needs—the need to be a responsible part of a larger system. It may show up in good ways or bad. Consider, for example, the way some teen-agers get led into delinquency. The maturing young man, who no longer is involved in family or school life, has a desperate need to identify with some other group, to which he will gladly give his loyalty and allegiance. Often the only organization to accept his offering will be a juvenile gang. Usually these gangs have their own elaborated rituals and practices and impose a rigid code of discipline. They meet the same need, although in a socially unacceptable way, as a well-organized corporation, union, or political party.

There are many sound methods for increasing involvement. I shall comment on only a few.

Communication—Down and Up

Knowledge has always created responsibility and involvement, especially when it expresses and communicates the genuine every-day concerns and sincere purposes of the organization.

In view of this potential it is unfortunate that all too often the only knowledge that a company gives its people is either openly propagandistic or purely social. The typical employee publication is full of articles on "Know Your Insurance Benefits" or something of that sort, and liberally embellished with pictures of babies and wedding scenes (sometimes weddings of 25 years ago). Whether such publications are well read or not I frankly do not know—or care—but I do know that articles dealing with more factual, busi-nesslike matters will be read—and will accomplish a much more worthwhile purpose. To illustrate from my own experience:

Each large supermarket contains half a dozen key executives—the manager and the department heads; and also there are a number of general supervisors. At certain seasons it is a problem to get a series of difficult bulletins, all on the same theme, to the right people in each of the supermarkets in the chain. Some years ago, in order to avoid over-looking anybody, we prepared a general sales bulletin of about 20 pages with different sections for each department, and sent a copy to all executives and supervisors.

We expected, of course, that the people in a given department would skip over the material which did not apply to them. Instead, everybody read everything. The fact that each department felt it was under public scrutiny added to the interest. Ever since, we have sought to give broad circulation to all sales and operating bulletins. We make no attempt to "glamorize" the material, yet it continues to be studied very closely. The zeal of the worker for simple statistical data on his part of the job is boundless.

Another important way of sharing knowledge is the communication *upward* of information from workers to management. Perhaps the important thing here is not the selection of a particular channel or method, but the effort to make the employee feel he can be heard when he wants to be.

This is primarily a matter of attitude. My own conviction is that here is the real and simple meaning of "human relations": the manager or supervisor must himself feel that his workers are human beings, and as such are naturally creative and cooperative. So he will instinctively want to listen to them and understand them—and they will feel that he does.

Local Self-Control

Management should turn over to each worker, group, and level every bit as much responsibility as is practical for controlling their own performance.

I realize, of course, that this is easier said than done. Developing even simple control systems requires talents not always possessed by workers—or by managers, either. (How many executives rely on their secretaries to organize their work?) Often there will be great capacity for "self-control," but the project will founder because of lack of ability to systematize, to set up the necessary techniques—the forms, papers, check lists, and so on.

Therefore, some management technician may have to do most of the original work of developing the system and then hand it over to be administered by the people on down the line—not simply delegating responsibility but showing how it works, answering questions about it, encouraging suggestions for modification, and in general trying to get the local people to take it over for their own use. When systems are developed on an upper-management level, they are often, for reasons of pride of authorship or sometimes just plain inertia, held in the upper level and administered downward. But if the organization is to function at anything near peak capacity—if all parts of it are to be really "alive"—I see no alternative to local control.

Areas of Free Choice

Involvement means nothing if one is involved as a cog in a machine. Boredom and fatigue set in quickly when people are without any area of free choice.

Some students of industrial organization have felt that morale under conditions of mass production can never be healthy because the worker makes only a small part of the whole product. I am not sure that this is true. Admittedly, if a man's job is to attach the heel onto the shoe, that and nothing else day in and day out, he could get more satisfaction out of making the whole shoe as his medieval (and somewhat romanticized) counterpart did. But assembly-line morale can still be improved importantly by introducing some area of choice or variety. It need *not* be a large area when related to the total work load. Perhaps the worker can select his best work rhythm, or be trained to act as his own inspector or to set up his own jigs, or be given the responsibility for the inventory of parts and supplies, or keep simple production statistics.

Consider the way a person turns to hobbies for recreation. If he is crafting a piece of woodwork, he follows the blueprints exactly, but alters his pace and stops occasionally, on his own decision, to measure and inspect. Much the same kind of freedom can, I believe, be given to company employees. To illustrate:

There are three steps in wrapping a package of self-service meat: weighing, printing the label, and wrapping. Among different girls there will be different aptitudes; one task calls for visual acuity, another for finger dexterity, and so on. Under "scientific management" bosses would assign the functions to separate individuals. Yet I have observed that when the five or six girls in a wrapping room are permitted to vary and rotate the tasks among themselves by their own plan or lack of plan, morale and production will improve.[2]

Leadership and the System

It is part of the argument here that the proper concern of management is for loyalty to—through involvement in—an operating system, not to persons or emotionally grounded concepts.

[2] See also William Foote Whyte, "Human Relations Theory—A Progress Report," *Harvard Business Review*, September-October 1956, p. 125.

Actually there are at least three possible levels of loyalty: (1) to the system; (2) to the leader as chief exponent of the system; and (3) to the leader as a person. The military life demonstrates examples of loyalty directly to a system rather than to a personal leader. As for illustrations of how a leader can represent the system, and represent it in the most vivid way:

(1) A recent *New York Times* review of a study of the conductor, Toscanini, ponders how this tyrannical, temperamental, and altogether extraordinary genius could hold the complete loyalty of associates. How could these devoted people keep their allegiance in the face of such vexations? The answer is that the response Toscanini got was earned because of his utter dedication to music and to his system of interpretation. His associates were also captives, in less degree, of this same dedication.

(2) Again, I remember a baseball team manager who, on an emotional level, was cordially despised by his players. Yet his complete fealty to the system, which also received their loyalty, was such that his players greatly respected his managership and achieved an enviable record of success.

As for the purely personal variety of leadership, while it is a valuable asset for a business, it offers nothing permanent on which an organization can build. Just because it is completely personal, it is evanescent and perishable. Furthermore, it cannot be learned and cannot be taught. While it can deepen the loyalty of a worker to the operating system, if he is already involved in it, it is not essential.

Certain practices common in industry today seem, quite unwittingly, to work against the development of sound leadership. We often aim wide of the mark when we seek to establish the position of the leader. One popular error is to subject the "head man" in a large company to a general public relations build-up, even though he might forever be only a name and a picture to most employees. Is it because of *him* that employees are expected to give their best?

An equal error is to magnify the leadership role of the foreman. Now, while a good foreman may elicit some personal loyalty, his authority and area are too clearly defined and restricted. He is a "subject" of the system and does not have the broad creative authority which would enable him to stand for—in a sense "be"—the system. To assume this responsibility a man must be able to exercise a considerable amount of discretion over the area under his control;

he must be a general officer, not a foreman.

Another leadership problem concerns the size of operating units. They must be large enough to support a general officer and not so large that they cease to be organic unities. In other words, the writ of the leader must be able to run through the entire organization. This may or may not be a problem. There are no size difficulties for the owner-managed shop of one hundred workers or for a ship at sea; in cases like this the immediate geographical environment is the proper unit. But what about the company with five hundred or a thousand or ten thousand scattered employees?

Significantly, larger firms which have practiced decentralization as a cardinal policy are the ones usually credited with the best management performance. This suggests that loyalty to the system, just because it is the system rather than to a personal leader, may be less vulnerable to the impersonalizing effects of distance and separation—and that it *is* something that can be developed through constructive management practices.

The chain food industry affords an interesting contrast that bears on this point:

The industry in New England has had no problem determining unit size; the store is obviously the basic unit. But a peculiar leadership pattern has evolved. There are two store managers, one responsible for the grocery and cashier departments, and the other for the meat and produce departments. There is no general store officer. At the same time, the control and authority of the visiting supervisors is considerable. There is a significant difference in rank, and customary practice requires both store managers to address the supervisor as "Mister."

By contrast, the food chains outside New England have generally followed the great example of Sears, Roebuck and Co. and J. C. Penney, which have made a considerable grant of authority to the one resident store manager. He is supervised less closely and considered more as an equal among equals in the management ranks. It is possibly significant that these other food chains have shown a more spectacular growth than seen in New England (Penn Fruit of Philadelphia and Food Fair Stores are notable examples). It is certainly significant that the New England chains are themselves slowly changing to the more sensible leadership policy.

What can so easily be forgotten is that leaders in local units, if they are to represent the system rather than function on the basis of personal loyalty, are all the more in need of clear authority. That is why staff men, who are a necessary corollary of decentralization, pose a threat; they often have such scope and power that they erode the position of the local manager.

Increasing complexity—cultural as well as industrial—has made technical specialists indispensable: personnel men, consultants, co-ordinators, expediters, and so forth. But maybe we have carried our zeal for their potentialities to excess and failed to develop the nonspecialized "whole" type of man who makes the best unit leader. The struggle for top management's favor has been uneven. Staff people are closer to headquarters, and usually their training gives them an advantage over the line officer in articulating and selling their programs. The dangers are obvious.

A worker in the ranks looks to his leader to make him part of the system, to adjust him to the system and the system to him, even to the extent of protecting him from the more drastic consequences of his own temporary and occasional lapses. (The leader, in this sense, humanizes the system rather than himself.) But if he is to see that his workers are treated with justice and sometimes with leniency, while not weakening the authority of his own lieutenants, the leader must be secure and confident in his own realm, free to act with creative flexibility.

MEN AND PRODUCTIVITY

American business has scored vast success with the glamorous techniques of mass advertising. We have created and spread the wants and desires that underpin our high standard of living, but so dazzled are we with this success that sometimes we erroneously apply these glittering devices of surface manipulation to employee management.

For example, we have taken the concept of "brand loyalty" out of context. We found it easy to think that employee loyalty might be generated by the same advertising techniques as those used for cigarettes and soap, forgetting that it can only be earned through effective leadership.

Manipulation—Mumbo Jumbo

We attempt to strike deep into the heart of a worker with the same mumbo jumbo which works so splendidly to sell tooth paste.

In all this we have overlooked an important distinction. When it comes to tooth paste, the worker does not really care; it is not a matter of moral conviction. People go along with the masquerade that says you should use a given brand because it will make you look like a certain movie star. It is a harmless form of play acting. But when it is a matter of a man's work, bearing on so much of his rational nature and so much of his daily life, then he must be treated like a man. To illustrate:

(1) Supermarkets hire many teen-agers as "bundle boys." In our organization we used to follow the popular practice of handing them a little propaganda piece, starting with the theme, "Little Leaks Sink Big Ships," and going on to tell how an unnecessary bag on the floor or a light left burning might put a busy supermarket out of business. The effect on the sophisticated adolescents was impressively negligible. We have found it better to attack waste simply because it is wrong—morally wrong—not because of economic consequences. We find that our young men appreciate the compliment to their self-respect.

(2) A brochure currently supplied by one of our largest trade associations seeks to motivate the newly hired teen-ager by stressing how essential the food business is, how many products come from mysterious lands overseas, how many fortunes have been made. This is supposed to inspire him to place the eggs on the top of the sack rather than on the bottom! Why isn't it both simpler and more effective just to tell him to pack the eggs this way so they don't get broken? Again, it is a compliment to assume that he would not want to do something that might keep the people who pay for the eggs from being able to use them when they get them home.

It has become a special passion with some firms to oversell the adventurous possibilities of employment in their organization. Now, there are—let us face it— many unglamorous and unromantic jobs in any industry. But must they be unashamedly veneered with a hypocritical camouflage, or else be ignored completely and relegated to the company Siberia?

How much better it would be to look for and to offer only the intrinsic rewards of work itself, and to recognize that as long as the task and the capacity are properly matched, satisfaction will arise spontaneously and will need no music, no flowers, no magic ritual to invoke it from on high. (As a matter of fact, this task of matching work load and individual capacity is too important to be abdicated to the personnel staff; it is one of the prime responsibilities of line management.)

I do not underestimate the potency of manipulative techniques. They can operate on a shallow level and induce a kind of "role playing" (shades of Bridey Murphy) or the same kind of play acting that secures a tooth paste manufacturer a major share of the market (shades of chlorophyll, dark green and light green). They can trespass into the emotional sphere, into the dark mind of the passions, and deliver a nation over to an Adolf Hitler. But these techniques are not proper tools for the building of a lucid, disciplined, intellectually loyal, and harmonious business community.

When we assume—and many of our professional personnel people do assume—that people really do not want to work and somehow must be motivated (which means manipulated) by sugar-coated pills, we not only injure their sense of integrity but do some of the very harm we are trying to avoid. There is an instinctive caution that makes people distrust techniques of manipulation when these are brought to bear on basic values. This distrust may carry over to much else that management stands for.

High Standards of Performance

Once management has created the best possible environment with the tools of organization and planning, and has done its best to involve the worker and to provide leadership, there remains the problem of productivity.

Some of us have wandered into the belief that the happy worker is necessarily the most productive worker. This is only a half truth, as some of the most important recent work done by industrial psychologists bears out. Worker happiness—you could use the word "satisfaction"—has only a negative relationship to productivity. Management will hardly ever get good performance from discontented people, but contentment in itself will not realize high performance.

Our concern for worker happiness can make us painfully sensitive to the work force's day-to-day shifts in mood and emotion, its instability and its ambivalences. We worry about griping—there is either too much or too little! We are hurt to discover that workers do not fully comprehend how the capitalist system *really* works and

how thin is the final margin of profit. We worry about loyalty—
do employees love the company or the union? We forget that a
man does not give his loyalty all of a piece or blindly. Good
workers respect both their company and their union. Their responses change day by day, and they will curse and praise first one
and then the other.

Sound personnel practices, or even sound "human relations," by
themselves do not solve the problem. Such practices are praise-
worthy and help remove the negative factors; as business managers
in a free society and as responsible human beings, we have an obligation to treat people humanely and with dignity. But let us do
this because it is civilized and fitting. Let us not distort our obligation with any half-true theory that we will be paid off with
greater productivity.

We can get productivity simply by asking for it, by insisting on
it, by setting high standards for management and employee alike.
For productivity is basically a moral problem. Management has a
moral obligation to society and to each worker to insist on peak
performance. The worker owes an obligation *to himself primarily*
to give his best. Of course, there is no "proof" for this ethic. You
will either accept it as "given," as fundamental like the law of
gravity, or you will reject it (along with the parable of the Workers
in the Vineyard) and search for some other touchstone in the elu-
sive fields of happiness, satisfaction, and motivation.

Management is often timid or diffident about using the basic
moral appeal and the old-fashioned concepts of right and wrong.
Possibly because management is so often called to justify its actions
in economic terms, we tend to rationalize what is essentially a
moral position under masquerades like "waste costs money" or
"productivity makes jobs."

But—I ask it again—do not workers respond more simply and
with less embarrassment to a more honest and less pretentious
statement? Consider yourself a new worker in an organization.
Your superior explains your responsibilities, without apologies or
romance, and concludes: "And now, sir, we want you to know—
and you'll be glad to know—that we have very high standards here.
We want from you the best you've got—the very best you can

deliver." Would such a challenge antagonize you? Would it not rather compliment your self-respect?

Conclusion

The industrial world is full of signs that work is valued as an end in itself. Certainly, on the management side, it seems clear that despite high income taxation and laments over the possible loss of initiative, business executives work harder than ever.

As for hourly paid workers, any experienced foreman will confirm that his good men do not work any harder when they receive a raise, but give their best regardless. This does not mean that management can escape its moral obligations to reward the virtuous. It means only that we should not confuse what we owe to the good worker as a matter of equity with the dynamism which drives him. Nor should we assume that he is less responsible than the manager, or driven less by the impulse to create and to cooperate.

Job satisfaction cannot be conditioned from above. Each employee—worker or executive—will learn it privately and for himself. Management can help best by demanding good work and spending less time stirring up shallow enthusiasms. Such an approach imposes stern responsibilities on management; it must maintain high standards for its own performance—for "housekeeping," for supplying and maintaining capital equipment, for planning, for discipline. The moral appeal is a strong and powerful one, but it must be applied sincerely, conscientiously, and self-critically if employers and employees are to grow toward a moral partnership and a strong sense of mutual obligations.

4.

Cynicism and Managerial Morality

By Benjamin M. Selekman*

One of the heartening signs of our times is the growing concern of businessmen with the ethical implications of their work. While science and secularism have undermined the influence of church and religion in so much of the community, businessmen have been struggling increasingly with the difficult task of squaring their function as wielders of economic power with the moral values of our Judaeo-Christian tradition. It is an exhilarating experience to see men engaged in the materialistic world of the market—in finance, production, selling, balancing profits and losses—so deeply involved in the moral issues of their workaday world.

Indeed, as one who moves in university circles, I am impressed with the greater concern with religious and moral values in business schools than among scholars in the humanities. The scholars are largely preoccupied not with substance but with technical scholarship—with the origin and evolution of ideas, with philological subtleties, with shades of meaning. Business schools, on the other hand, are faced continuously with the necessity of helping executives, in training and in practice, to make decisions involving the equities of employees, customers, government representatives, and trade union officials. Almost always, justice and fair dealing spring up as considerations, even though efficiency and profits are the explicit goals.

* Mr. Selekman is Kirstein professor of labor relations at the Harvard Business School.

A personal experience brought this home to me clearly:

On reading two articles of mine,[1] a noted scholar in the philosophy of religion turned to me and said, "You know, you write with moral fervor!" He did not mean this altogether as a compliment; to him scholarship is technical and does not deal with values. By contrast, I feel—as do so many others—that one cannot study the tug of power between men and men, or between institutions and institutions, without becoming involved in ethical implications. This is especially so in these critical days when naked power and its manipulation have been elevated to a major strategy in so many parts of the world—almost completely replacing old-fashioned diplomacy.

If teachers of business become thus involved, how much greater is the involvement of the practicing businessman! Living in an atmosphere of misunderstanding and even hostility, he is almost under the necessity of pondering ethical implications willy-nilly when making decisions. Indeed, this may constitute his major challenge: how to be efficient, make profits, *and* observe moral values. Elsewhere I have called this perpetual tension "the technical 'must' versus the ethical 'ought.' "[2]

ROOTS OF CYNICISM

At the same time, however, one must also take note of a strain of cynicism in the business world—occasionally amounting to a latter-day type of Machiavellianism—especially in relation to government, trade unions, intellectuals, and even difficult people within management's own plants who seem to thwart cherished objectives.

Pressures and Temptations

Cynicism does not in itself completely identify this attitude. It also has elements of distrust, fear, and hostility. Surely it is not the quality of the "gentle cynic" who withdraws from life and laughs at the frailties of the human race. It is rather a pervasive suspicion which leads to questionable behavior, which in turn often boom-

[1] "Is Management Creating a Class Society?" *Harvard Business Review*, January-February 1958, p. 37; and "Trade Unions—Romance and Reality," *Harvard Business Review*, May-June 1958, p. 76.
[2] Sylvia and Benjamin Selekman, *Power and Morality in a Business Society* (New York, McGraw-Hill Book Company, Inc., 1956), pp. 3-96.

erangs on business itself. For at times cynicism reaches the extreme of writing off all politicians and labor leaders as self-seeking, if not corrupt; and so it follows that the only practical recourse for management is to enter into deals, collusive arrangements, and backdoor agreements, and to seek and retain the right "go-between." In the end all this frequently brings about the corruption exposed by legislative committees from time to time. The revelations of the McClellan Committee are a case in point.

How is one to reconcile such cynicism with a stimultaneous emphasis on moral values? Can it be that businessmen, smarting under long and severe attack, have now become so sure of their own rectitude that they look with contempt on those who do not go along with them? And if this is so, may it not follow that, unless executives come to grips with this drift toward cynicism and distrust, they are in danger of forfeiting whatever respect they have gained? One thing seems sure: they may as well face the fact that they will never again enjoy the opportunity for unilateral decision making. That day is gone forever. They must count on continuous opposition—and hopefully, as time goes by, on an intelligent, informed opposition—from the labor unions, farmers, consumer groups, reformers, and government agencies.

Another reason for this negative attitude may be that since so much of a modern executive's daily life is taken up with negotiating and bargaining for material gains, his path is bestrewn with temptation to take advantage of his superior economic position, as well as his greater knowledge, skill, and experience in the intimate matters of corporate life. Not infrequently he is under pressure to outsmart his opposite number in the union or a government agency; and he has a natural desire to outmaneuver any opponent who is trying to best him. In fact, the temptation to get the jump on such an adversary is almost overwhelming.

Thus, cynicism finds in such a bargaining atmosphere a fertile soil in which to survive and thrive.

Morality in Politics

Similarly, because bargaining and trading are such important aspects of politics, a cynical attitude prevails toward political activity. Indeed, by convention we tolerate a double standard of morality—a public posture on the highest moral level and a private life where deals and bargains are made. Since limits exist on the actual officeholders, it is the party leaders who really do the trading, the bargaining, and the making of deals. They raise the money necessary to keep the party going, and frequently make implicit promises of preferment, or at least an inside track of good will with the administration, if and when it comes to office.

We leave politics to the "bosses." We shrug our shoulders as if to say, "What is the use?" And so an atmosphere of cynicism develops. Businessmen can hardly claim exemption from succumbing to this drift. Indeed, they have a ready excuse at hand; they have to be "practical." The argument seems to make so much sense that we may even look the other way when we see a leading executive noted for the highest integrity acquiescing in the behavior of a dubious, if not corrupt, politician for fear of reprisal on his own business interests. We forget—as probably he does—that in matters of character and morality one cannot be cynical and moral at the same time. Once he takes a negative attitude toward human beings, it becomes difficult, if indeed not impossible, for him to inspire men with confidence in the integrity of his leadership.

DEALING WITH UNIONS

When it comes to dealing with trade unions, fear intensifies cynicism. For a great many years corporations resisted and fought unions with every possible weapon—from influencing town and county officials to keep union organizers out as trespassers, to refusing unions permission to hold public meetings, to arresting union leaders as disturbers of the peace, and finally to mobilizing special police or sheriffs with weapons to "shoot it out." (Labor, too, has resorted to all kinds of dubious activity in trying to "reach" public officials, as well as in mobilizing its "military" forces.) Cynicism easily becomes the natural attitude for justifying this kind of strategy.

During the late 1930's most corporations finally realized that trade unionism could no longer be held off. The acceptance of the inevitable was, however, mainly reluctant and, once again, cynical. The New Deal and Fair Deal were blamed, and Roosevelt, Perkins, and Truman were projected as the villains responsible for the invasion of property rights—the sit-downs, mass picketing, and other manifestations of raw power that accompanied the "explosion" in organizing activity.

Obviously, the new unions were bound to be crude and headstrong. Some of the leaders were dedicated men desiring to improve the lot of their fellow workers, but some were self-seeking, some corrupt, and some sympathetic with Communism. It was bound to take time for these unions to make the transition from a fighting to an administrative stage, and for the emergence of a leadership adequate to the requirements of newly acquired power and prestige.

Machiavellianism

The temptation at the time was to try to make deals with those leaders considered "sensible," and/or to weaken and divide the unions and their leadership. In the prevailing climate all this was understandable because recognition of unions did not come as a voluntary act, but was imposed on company after company by economic and political power. Resentment and a latent desire to be punitive followed. Instead of realizing that what was called for was a long-range strategy founded on a sound moral basis, many managements let cynicism become their guiding philosophy. In so doing they were sure to give hostage to conflict and hostility, and sometimes even corruption.

By playing Machiavelli one may think he assures himself the upper hand. He may even buy some immediate peace, or rather a semblance of peace. But only for a little while; the reckoning is sure to come. To illustrate:

At the end of World War II General Motors Corporation did not have in its midst a "specialist" in making deals like Harry Bennett of Ford Motor Company, nor did its strategy call for such "talent." Instead, it followed the age-old, cynical, Machiavellian formula of "divide and rule."

Stung by Walter P. Reuther's aggressiveness and militancy in the prolonged strike of 1945–1946, when he proposed a "look at the books," the management concluded negotiations first with the Communist-dominated United Electrical Workers (UE), though it did not represent nearly as many General Motors employees as did Reuther's United Auto Workers (UAW). However, James Matles of the UE and his fellow travelers "cooperated" eagerly with the General Motors management and agreed to a less costly "package" than that demanded by Reuther and the UAW. The Communist leaders were most anxious to cut their archenemy, Reuther, down to size. In fact, UE and General Motors between them succeeded in leaving Reuther practically no recourse but to follow along and accept the UE package for his union, both in 1946 and 1947.

Thus, a major bastion of American capitalism played hand in hand with Communist "party liners"—both bent, though for different reasons, on preventing Reuther from rising to a place of power in the labor movement. Significantly, the settlement made in 1947 by General Motors and the UE became the pattern for the rest of the country. Indeed, it looked for a while as if the leading capitalist corporation and the leading Communist-dominated union would jointly become the dominant pattern-makers for American industry.

Need the lesson be pointed up? Cynicism and Machiavellianism have a way of spawning their corrosive course far past immediate tactics to eat away at such fundamental values as human freedom and dignity. Once the damage has been done, it takes almost a superhuman effort of the most intelligent management to make amends. For labor leaders and union members become cynical, too, when they hear corporations speak about the free enterprise system and the threat of Communism to our cherished interests.

A corporation of the stature of General Motors was bound to realize before long that Machiavellian stratagems led only to Pyrrhic victories. In 1948 it broke new paths with its pattern-setting proposal that wages should be based on the dual principles of increased productivity and fluctuations in cost of living. Before long this too became the pattern for American industry.

The moral becomes obvious: a corporation of the magnitude of General Motors lets the whole nation down if it resorts to cynical strategies, just as it breaks new paths for progressive stability when it follows ethical goals. In these matters, as in personal relations, the larger and more powerful we are, the more we must look on ourselves as "our brother's keeper." What is good for the country *must* be good for the great corporation.

Boulwareism

An outstanding example of cynicism is the managerial strategy represented by what has come to be known as Boulwareism, named after a General Electric vice president, Lemuel R. Boulware. It is based on these principles:

> Management knows best what should be done for its employees.
>
> It should therefore make up its mind prior to any negotiation what should be the maximum offer.
>
> It should refuse to recede from or alter this offer in any substantial way.
>
> It should take a strike, if necessary, and hold out until the union capitulates.

In a more recent address Boulware severely indicted unions (without making any exceptions) for using force instead of persuasion at the bargaining table, for developing a strategy of "political bargaining," and for "promoting the something-for-nothing, inflationary, foreign socialist brand of anti-business economics. . . ." He called on businessmen to rally on the political field to defeat union leaders. He congratulated Arizona businessmen for having been active in the enactment of a right-to-work law, and told them that "a very important factor in General Electric's decision favoring Arizona over the other contenders for our computer business was the combination of the fact that you *do* have a right-to-work law and the fact that *a growing majority* of the citizens are so obviously coming to appreciate and support voluntarism as opposed to compulsion in union membership."[3]

Surely it is unfair to lump all unions under a blanket indictment! Corporations have suffered so much from being on the receiving end of that kind of strategy that it is difficult to understand a similar tactic by a spokesman for one of the country's leading companies. Could it be evidence of a latent prejudicial attitude toward trade unions?

Under certain situations a strategy of containment may be a sound one—when dealing with a new and undisciplined union, or a Communist-dominated one, or one with irresponsible leaders, or if demands are so excessive as to threaten the competitive position of a company. However, if the aim is to "cut a union down to size," to beat union leadership to the punch, then indeed the strategy is

[3] "Politics . . . the Businessman's Biggest Job in 1958," given before the annual meeting of the Phoenix Chamber of Commerce, Phoenix, Arizona, May 21, 1958.

tantamount to a Machiavellian use of power to discredit and, if possible, to destroy the union. It denies workers adequate and competent representation, for such tactics will never afford leaders an opportunity for development and growth. Indeed, the most serious moral defect of Boulwareism lies precisely in the fact that it deprives a human institution of the opportunity to grow in maturity and responsibility.

The labor movement is bound to take on increasing importance as time goes on. While in the foreseeable future of this country we are not likely to face a labor party as in Free Europe, trade unions and their adherents nevertheless play an important role in affairs of state as well as of industry. The best way for union members and leaders to acquire knowledge of the complex economic, political, and social factors at work is to learn through the negotiation and administration of agreements. But Boulwareism affords them little or no opportunity to undergo such an experience. It presents them with a "take it or leave it" ultimatum. The consequent danger may be a lethargic rank and file, with the radical, the impractical, or the militant rising to leadership; or, worse, the corrupt and predatory may "muscle in" and take over. So we may face, if Boulwareism spreads, the risk of firmly established and powerful unionism without responsible membership and leadership—an ominous eventuality.

Joint Operation

Moreover, is it not a fallacy to assume, as does Boulwareism, that management can look out for employee welfare better than can union officials? In an age of specialization, management must have as its primary concern the economic health of the business as shown in profits; unions, the welfare of their members. The latter is not an easy job in a competitive world where industry must continually adjust to new technologies, shifting markets, or periods of recession, and where the workmen must be transferred, furloughed, demoted, and even discharged.

In truth, modern industry is a combined operation for management and labor. It is arrogant for either group to assume that it has a key to superior wisdom or morality. They represent adverse as well as common interests. While they may differ as to the distribution of proceeds, they agree on the desirability of maximum productivity. And everyone is the greater gainer when both mutual and conflicting interests are recognized and the parties gather around the table to negotiate the best possible agreement in terms of efficiency as well as of social justice.

Admittedly, the temptation to pursue the course of Boulwareism is strong. Labor leaders have to engage in a great deal of political maneuvering to get their members to accept settlements reached with management, and politics of this kind leads management to become impatient, if not cynical. Managers forget that union leaders, while they have behind them a political machine, must somehow meet expectancies which are often far beyond the realm of the possible. It takes adroitness to persuade union members who pay dues and elect officials to accept a smaller wage than they thought was "in the bag" during the prenegotiation campaign. Even as skilled and strong a leader as Reuther is confronted every once in a while with a "revolt."

One can easily become impatient when faced with the need to make commitments on cost and delivery while being kept in suspense by all this "politicking." How tempting it is to adopt Boulwareism as a strategy and thus be in a position to call the shots! Yet to do so is to imply a cynical attitude toward democracy and its capacity to develop sober, responsible leadership. In these human matters, as in strictly business ones, management must be willing to take risks.

Outside "Fixers"

It comes as a shock, from time to time, to learn that a corporation of repute has betrayed its own standards of ethical behavior by accepting the standards of "fixers." What leads businessmen to enter into deals with men of questionable character in the hope of thus obtaining "peaceful" industrial relations?

The fall from grace usually has its beginning when a company, after successfully fending off a union, finally faces the necessity of coming to terms with it. It then turns to a lawyer or a consultant who "knows" his way about. The very act of turning to such a man is itself symptomatic of fear or cynicism, or both, and these attitudes are in danger of being sharpened as managers are exposed to the way the outsider "helps" them.

Admittedly, lawyers have an important role to play in preparing for negotiations, in participating in the actual bargaining sessions, and in drafting the clauses of the final contract. But these are technical matters. In *policy making,* management must hew out its own course; it must take responsibility for ethical standards, strategy, and tactics. Counsel should be around only to help think through and carry out the policies decided on within the legal framework of state and nation. If the lawyer is closely identified with the management as a wise associate who has helped to guide the corporation amidst the pressures of a changing world, well and good. There are many lawyers of this type who are a real asset. But the vital decisions as to ethical standards, just as those involving costs and competition, should always remain with management.

A Weak Union

Here is an example of what happens when management turns over too much responsibility to the lawyer and does not think through the problems itself:

A blue-chip company was involved—as outstanding for its product as for its public service. A strike had occurred in one of its plants. To take stock and avoid, if possible, the repetition of such shutdowns, a conference of central and plant personnel was called to which I was invited.

It turned out that a major problem was the weakness of the union. It had been proving a failure as a means of channeling employee attitudes to supervision, or of affording supervisors an avenue for discussing critical problems affecting productivity and employee morale.

It did not take long to discover the reason behind this failure. Among those present was the company's counsel. He dominated the discussion and always came up with a ready, "simple" answer. Whenever one of his clients was subject to a union campaign, he said, he was usually called by labor leaders with the offer of a good "deal" if he would get the company to sign up for a union shop and the checkoff. These union leaders, he added, were primarily interested not in the men but in the "deals." He did not think that there was much hope in any effort to arouse interest in the union, which now enjoyed bargaining rights.

Later inquiry revealed that he was the very same lawyer who had brought this union in through a backdoor agreement with its president during the New Deal days when organizing campaigns were taking place all over the country.

Actually, it is not fair to put all of the blame on the lawyer. In the beginning, the company's management had wanted a weak, compliant union. It failed to see that this was at best a short-lived expedient. All sorts of problems began arising daily in its various plants which involved employee relationships, but local executives had no one with whom to discuss them. The union president who had made the deal was located far from any of the plants, and knew little about what was going on.

To management's credit, it realized that its previous course of action had not been paying off, and it commenced working on a more realistic approach.

The point is that once a union comes into a plant, it is to the interest of management to have it active. Otherwise, supervisors have no one with whom to handle the problems which are bound to arise from day to day.

"Buying" Union Officials

Another aspect of cynicism in union relations is to tempt into the management fold the man who shows ability and aggressiveness as a union official. "Why not put this man on our side," executives may say. "If he is good enough for the union, he certainly ought to be good enough for us."

Such thinking fails to take into consideration the consequences of depriving a union of leadership. To hire away an effective union official is to create a vacuum. A less able person is likely to be elected as successor; the men may flounder around without anyone to guide them through the maze of economic, technical, and social problems that inevitably arise from day to day. And so again management finds itself baffled because of lack of adequate representation of its employees.

Another point overlooked frequently is that the transition from one role to another, in which a man virtually changes sides, is fraught with the danger of misunderstanding and suspicion. He runs the risk of being suspected of being a turncoat—for money. And if (as often happens) he is appointed to a position in personnel, in which as the administrator of managerial policies he may have to take positions contrary to the very ones he fought for in his union role, then the potential damage to confidence in the integrity of management is great.

This is not to say that an employee who becomes active in union affairs should never be promoted to a management position; there are times when it is a good idea. But the move should be made only after full discussion. If management still favors it then, care should be taken in the early stages not to put the erstwhile union official in a position where he has to oppose the very union which he has left, such as leading the management in negotiating a new agreement, or representing it in an arbitration procedure, or acting as a witness against his former brethren. Of course, the temptation is overwhelming to do that very thing—to turn over to the former labor official the job of making his erstwhile brethren "reasonable." To give in to it, however, is to imply to the people in and outside the plant an underlying attitude of cynicism.

A related form of temptation—equally important to resist—is the hiring of a local celebrity or politician as personnel or labor relations director. The elevation of Harry Bennett by the elder Henry Ford is an extreme example. To be sure, an ex-mayor or other erstwhile public officeholder may know how to manipulate and "fix" troublesome officials in government or in the union. But whether or not bribes are passed (very often they are not), the reputation of the company becomes blemished as the suspicion spreads, not only inside the mill gates but also throughout the entire community.

DEALING WITH INDIVIDUALS

Frequently one finds a management cynical not only in over-all dealings with unions but also in the handling of individual cases, particularly when settlements made in the front office are not accepted at the shop level. Such behavior provokes executives to comment that the union men cannot be trusted, that they are "just politicians," whereas the truth of the matter is that frequently the difficulties inherent in the human situation are of a dimension not easily disposed of by a "settlement."

Injustice to One Man . . .

Here, from a case I became familiar with several years ago, is the kind of thing that can happen when one man is treated in a way which his fellow workers consider unjust:

A veteran employee whom I shall call "Andy" was an all-around welder who could work with electric, acetylene, and other tools. Once the high-est rated man in his group, he had worked for the company for about thirty years. In his early years, when welding was not nearly as extensively used as now, he had helped train novitiates in the job. Over the years, Andy had always received the highest incentive rate.

During the war, when welding superseded riveting, the company decided, with the consent of the union, to develop a job-classification plan for welders. Andy felt, as did his "buddies," that he would always get the highest rate no matter what new jobs arose; in fact, he thought that management had made such a promise to him.

Subsequent to the completion of job classification, however, two higher rates were established to cover welding on heavy construction outside the shop. Andy continued to remain *in* the shop, where he had always been, and complained that he suffered an injustice in the form of a wage cut.

When the grievance could not be adjusted in the department, it went to the top executives at plant level and the corresponding union officials. There a settlement was reached. The company agreed to pay Andy the difference between what he had earned and what he would have earned had he gone out on the construction jobs, even though management could find no one who remembered promising him the highest rate. The difference for fifteen months amounted to sixty dollars. Andy was sent a check with the understanding that the grievance was settled; henceforth, if he wished, he could continue to earn the highest rate by taking on the jobs outside the shop.

. . . Breeds Cynicism in Others

But was the grievance settled? Not by a long shot! In fact, it was finally appealed to arbitration, and this is what happened:

Both company and union had failed to sense that the insignificant amount of sixty dollars did not touch the heart of the matter. Worker after worker protested that Andy had been wronged; that he was entitled to and should receive the highest rate. They spoke of him as a responsible leader both for them and the company. It was a disgrace, they insisted, to demote him now—yes, to "degrade" him.

Management admitted that at one time Andy constituted a "one-man" department, but argued that the company now had a diversified crew and any number of welders to turn to for whatever work might be needed. Andy *could* still earn the highest rate if he would go out and work on heavy construction jobs, management pointed out.

Since Andy insisted on remaining in the shop, he had really become little more than what the company classified as a "handy man," handing out glass and rods to the welders. The appellation of "handy man" outraged the other workers. They charged that the company was discarding a valuable, old employee after having got the best out of him for years. Did not management realize that, as a teacher, Andy always stayed in the shop? That was where he was expected to be for whatever emergency might arise. To expect him now in his late years to climb construction trestles was shameful!

Thus, the settlement made in the front office by top company and union officials had been rejected at the shop level because, in the eyes of the ranks, a cynical evaluation had been placed on Andy and his contribution over the years.

The union officials next found themselves in an embarrassing dilemma when they failed to get the rank and file to accept their settlement with management. So they, too, resorted to a questionable stratagem. They now argued that the foreman and superintendent were showing hostility to, and discriminating against, Andy because he had complained; that the agreement was therefore not being carried out in good faith. This effort to reopen the case made managers all the more cynical; they now were quite sure that the union representatives were not trustworthy.

Thus cynicism finally destroyed a natural foundation for strengthening morality. Instead of building a richer relationship on the human values which surrounded Andy and his fellow welders, and in this way elevating the technical importance of welding to the moral heights of a "guild," the episode ended in bitterness and frustration. Those who were cynical became more so, and those (particularly the riveters) who started out with good will ended up distrusting both company and union.

Old Workers on New Jobs

A note of impatience merging into snideness not infrequently creeps into discussions relating to older employees. I have sat in meetings where plant executives threw their hands up, baffled as to what to do with older employees, once skilled and valued men but no longer up to handling newer, more complicated tools and processes. As long as manual skill and judgment are the chief requirement, they are "tops." But when, with increasing mechanization, it comes to handling complex, continuous processes with close tolerances, their responses are no longer flexible enough. The foreman or engineer has to stand by to step into the breach when anything goes wrong.

Beyond physical factors, one confronts here what is without doubt a major psychological difficulty—whether an older man of skill and craftsmanship can ever adjust himself to increasing automation; indeed, whether he ever really accepts it. Nevertheless, if management truly means what it says when it talks about human dignity as basic in American morality, it surely cannot afford to look down its nose at highly valued men who made their contribution in their times to the growth of a business.

To be sure, local plant managers are often on the spot. Maximum productivity is expected from new equipment in which large capital investments have been made. If they fail, plant executives are called to task. They are thus caught between the human problems of the older people and the "hardheaded" pressures of top management. Obviously the balance of power is on the side of the latter.

It is therefore only natural to become impatient with the difficulties of older workers. From impatience it is but a step to cynicism. They are mentioned with condescension. They are moved from job to job until they become handy men—with lower status and less pay. What is overlooked is the impact of such treatment on the plant community. Since reverence for the aged is a Judaeo-Christian virtue, one which is all the more to be observed if the elders have in their time made a contribution to the life of the community, any management that handles a middle-aged employee even remotely in a spirit of cynicism thereby forfeits respect for itself.

Justification for Discipline

An underlying cynical attitude leads at times to excessively harsh discipline, justified occasionally by a spurious mixture of technical and moral arguments. For example:

An employee holding the highest position in his department was demoted three rungs, ostensibly for failure to observe the rule of notifying his foreman at home when a breakdown occurred. The demotion was so drastic as to obviate any possibility of even a temporary reassignment to the highest post if, on any day, the new incumbent failed to turn up.

The case was appealed to arbitration. Management argued that the breakdown and loss of production was not the only reason for the demotion. In the past the employee had failed both to observe safety regulations and also to maintain harmony among his crew.

The clear and undisputed fact was that not until the event of the breakdown and the consequent loss of production was the severe penalty imposed. No regard was given to the man's long service, stretching over thirty years, nor to the fact that he had served in the top job for nine years and supervised a crew of a dozen men operating complicated machine tools, nor to the fact that he was one of the highest production men in the mill. Clearly he was without malice or ill will to his men or the company. He was almost naïve as he expressed "love" for his job.

Indeed, if any fault was to be found, it was his overzealousness for production, which led him to drive his men and occasionally to neglect safety regulations. But it should not have been overlooked that the prevailing incentive system put all the emphasis on production; the greater the output, the higher the take-home pay.

What bothered me most about the case was that at the hearing management based its defense primarily on a lofty "human relations" argument that the man had failed to secure a cooperative spirit in his crew and, on occasion, had jeopardized their life and limb. To use a moral argument to justify a questionable demotion precipitated by a costly failure in production evidenced, to my way of thinking, a cynical attitude—cynical toward the employee as well as toward the arbitration process. No one seriously believed that the man had willfully failed to observe the rules of decent human conduct; the only issue was a purely materialistic one—the cost of machine breakdown and output.

As a matter of fact, though my award called for his reinstatement, so acute was his humiliation and sense of injustice that before long he quit.

Use of Technicalities

An underlying attitude of cynicism is also, I believe, responsible for an overlegalistic handling of human situations at the sacrifice of individual equity. Let me illustrate with two grievance cases in one plant:

A machinist was allowed to take Wednesday and Thursday off one week in lieu of part of his regular vacation; color photography was his hobby, and he wanted to take pictures of a flower show that was in town. He returned to work on Friday.

Normally Saturday was a day off; when worked, it was paid at overtime.

The machinist came to work Saturday at the request of his foreman, who signed his time card crediting him with time and a half. His paycheck included the extra money for that day. Shortly thereafter, however, the auditors ran across this item, judged it an overpayment because the man had not worked the five previous days as stipulated by the union agreement, and deducted it from his next paycheck.

This case happened during a period of full employment, when a skilled man could easily pick up a job on Saturday at a premium rate. The machinist came in to work to help out his foreman, and both understood that overtime would be paid. In fact, after the deduction had been made, the foreman went to the management and urged that it be restored. Management, however, refused. It became a grievance, and eventually went to arbitration. It appeared that it was not so much the money involved (under ten dollars, actually) as the formal legalism of the contract and the danger of establishing a precedent that the company was concerned with. In its desire to press a technical advantage, instead of making an exception, it overlooked the equities of the machinist as well as the relationship between him and the foreman.

In the second case management had allowed a fitter a make-up rate on special-order work, which consumed about half of his time. This practice virtually guaranteed him incentive earnings instead of the guaranteed minimum day rate when working on nonincentive jobs. Again, an alert auditor scanning the payroll concluded that under the contract negotiated five years prior it was not necessary to pay any make-up or special rates; in fact, the practice was prohibited.

As of a certain date, therefore, management stopped paying the fitter his extra bonus. The result was that he lost, on the average, about fifteen cents an hour every day in comparison with his usual incentive earnings. Management made no attempt to work out an incentive rate for the special work (it maintained it could not be done), or to find some other legalistic formula by means of which it could continue the customary practice of paying this man his average incentive earnings (legalism *can* be made to work toward equitable goals as well as toward denial of equity).

It turned out that the fitter was the only one in the crew skilled enough to do what amounted to a tailored job on joints required for bridges and other types of construction. Thus, in a sense he was doing management a favor by taking on these assignments. Under the circumstances both he and his friends were deeply offended that instead of a reward, he should actually suffer a loss.

But the argument of the company was that just because it had paid an extra bonus to this man for five years was no reason why it should continue to "overpay" him. Should it be penalized, it asked blandly at the arbitration hearing, for either carelessness or generosity up to this time?

The sense of injustice became more acute when the company interposed a technical procedural bar to my making a decision on the merits of the case: it argued that arbitration was barred on the ground of "untimeliness." The union had failed to appeal the case to arbitration within the time limits specified in the contract. This had happened because of the inexperience of the full-time union official, who was new on his job; this was the first time he had ever invoked arbitration. He had thought the minutes of the prior joint grievance meeting as recorded by the company in error and returned them for correction. He was of the opinion that he could still appeal to arbitration after the parties had agreed to the correctness of the record. He was wrong; the wording of the contract was clear. But it was an error growing out of inexperience.

The importance of upholding the procedural aspects of law is not to be denied. But obviously one has to use discrimination. Where equities are so compelling, as in the case of this fitter, and where inexperience accounted for the lapse in the procedure of appealing his case, to press a legal advantage which would shut off even consideration of merits was tantamount to depriving the situation of all moral value.

As arbitrator in these two cases, I found for the men, frankly basing my award on the equities of the cases, although the literal wording of the agreements did uphold management. Even though I went out of my way to make it clear that I was making an exception which was not to be considered a precedent, I received a withering letter from the company protesting that my decision exemplified a double standard of conduct—one for the company, and one for the union!

Distrust of Intellectuals

One of the most serious manifestations of cynicism is the attitude of distrust toward "intellectuals," especially toward the unorthodox and the nonconformist. The intellectual may be no more radical than Professor (now Justice) Felix Frankfurter, but rather an old-fashioned liberal in the Holmes and Brandeis tradition. If, however, he advised and assisted in shaping something that was called a New Deal program, or was moved earlier to challenge the ways of justice as meted out to two immigrant Italians, he is in danger of losing his standing as the result of the battering of influential alumni—many of them businessmen!

The shrieks of intolerance are all the more strident if a professor was naïve enough, in the flush of youthful idealism, to join anything like a Communist cell, or just to attend meetings where Communists congregated.

Indeed, the attitude of many businessmen toward the intellectual is contradictory, if not almost schizoid. On the one hand, corporations welcome eagerly the findings of scholars which contribute to technological advance or to a better understanding of human behavior. On the other hand, in their rejection of the intellectuals, they create a hostile climate and thus undermine the very creativity essential for a progressive technology and improved human relations. They forget that when things are new and in a pioneering stage, scholarly theories and findings may sound offensive and even shocking. People do not like to be disturbed from their familiar moorings, whether they be physical, social, or intellectual. The story of Galileo is an oft-told tale but, alas, each generation forgets it.

Can we afford to continue such a hostile atmosphere in face of the cataclysm hovering over mankind? Indeed, even if we surmount the present danger, the only wealth and power that counts in the end for peace as for war is derived from the intellectual capital accumulated by scholarship in science and the humanities. To maintain, under such circumstances, a distrustful and cynical attitude toward scholars is to cut the very ground from under the most creative men.

Beyond the current crisis is the long-range challenge of coming to grips with the destructive potential in man: his capacity for hate like that for love, his reaching out for evil as he does for good. For this purpose, too, we must turn to our scholars in the social and medical sciences, in the humanities, and in the theological seminaries in order to keep building, revitalizing, and enriching the intellectual, moral, and aesthetic resources of mankind to sustain and guide us through our perplexities.

SANCTIONS OF AUTHORITY

Much has been said and written about the sources of authority that give management its right to direct men. It has long since been recognized that authority based on rights of property, though controlling in courts of law, carries little weight in the daily life of a corporation. Thus it has become fashionable to say that authority comes, not from above, but "from below."

Importance of Moral Posture

But what is it that comes "from below"? The most potent factor, I submit, is the moral atmosphere projected by the chief executive and his management group. No one can exercise power effectively these days without conveying the conviction that he does so responsibly, that is, with justice. Since management combines in itself the usual three functions of government—legislative, executive, judiciary—and since it is self-perpetuating, it constitutes a tremendous holder of power.

Because of our democratic, Judaeo-Christian society, the legality of property rights must give way to consent. But how does one obtain consent? By the conviction that power is controlled by and directed toward ethical goals. It is not the words that are important. It is attitude and behavior that convey the omnipresence of a moral posture. In this sense, authority does not come from below but rather stems from the integrity of the entire business as a human institution fraught with moral values.

A cynical attitude is in direct contradiction to all this. Indeed, by definition it implies distrust of human motives; it is bound to breed suspicion. And so individuals, be they supervisors, technicians, or hourly workers, do not feel comfortable with a cynical leader. The only recourse then available to the executive is to use power in the form of fear and intimidation.

For a while, during the nineteenth and early twentieth centuries, fear may have been effective; the industrial scene was influenced by such conditions as surplus labor, mass immigration, and nothing but private charity between work and starvation. In recent years, however, a host of protective agencies have sprung up to prevent arbitrary discipline or discharge, and to provide maintenance on at least a modest level until another job is obtained. Even more, the whole moral and social climate has so changed that no longer can a "boss" govern for any length of time by threats of punishment. Thus, from a practical point of view, since management cannot rule by force, cynicism destroys the main sanction for authority, for it undermines man's faith in man.

If anyone thinks I am overly idealistic, let him recall the "big" men he has worked under. Was it not confidence in their sense of justice and fair play as well as in their technical ability that made them the leaders they became in their respective industries and communities? Moreover, if it be true that the contemporary crisis of society is a moral one; if it be true that men are losing faith in the old ways of doing things, and turning more and more to powerful politicians; if it be true that man is trying to escape from freedom into the arms of all-powerful government—then what alternative is there but to generate the faith that rises from a morally responsible attitude in the everyday exercise of authority?

Cynicism erodes inner strength. If one is to handle large and complex responsibilities, as do most business executives, one has to be fortified by belief in the people who surround him. One does not receive confidence unless he gives it to others. It is these imponderable elements that give vitality to an institution as a living community of men, that call forth effort beyond the line of duty, and that make one want to excel in all things.

Conclusion

I started off this article by underlining the significance of the social and ethical posture assumed by American business during the past quarter century. Let me repeat that, outside of church circles, I find nowhere so much moral ferment as among corporation executives and teachers of business. This development makes it doubly important for managers to be alert to the dangers of cynicism. With its potential for destruction of the very values we seek to foster in American industrial society.

For cynicism is all too prevalent. Unless checked, it may destroy whatever faith people may be developing in the integrity of bankers, manufacturers, merchants, and other business groups in their respective communities. It may isolate the centers of a moral renaissance and abort the efforts of leaders to raise the social consciousness of management. Cynicism is negation. To the cynic, man is basically and always selfish, self-aggrandizing, and exploitative of his fellow man. Surely this is completely contrary to what thoughtful businessmen assume about human nature when they emphasize social and ethical goals.

All this is not without significance in the contemporary world-wide crisis. Let us remember that the Communist imperialists condemn capitalism and democracy as doomed precisely because they are inherently cynical, selfish, and exploitative. Surely, as we reach out for friends and allies, we can ill afford to play into the hands of our enemies. And within the nation, it is well to put our house in order.

5.

"Skyhooks"

(With Special Implications for

Monday through Friday)

By O. A. Ohmann*

During the last several years, while my principal job assignment has been management development, I have become increasingly impressed with the importance of intangibles in the art of administration. With the managerial revolution of the last generation and the transition from owner-manager to professional executive, there has appeared a growing literature on the science and art of administration. A shift in emphasis is noticeable in these writings over the past thirty years.

Following the early engineering approach typified by the work of Frederick Taylor and others, there next developed a search for the basic principles of organization, delegation, supervision, and control. More recently, as labor relations became more critical, the emphasis has shifted to ways of improving human relations. The approach to the problems of supervisory relationships was essentially a manipulative one. Textbooks on the techniques of personnel management mushroomed. Still later it became more and

* Mr. Ohmann is assistant to the president, Standard Oil Company of Ohio.

more apparent that the crux of the problem was the supervisor himself, and this resulted in a flood of "how to improve yourself" books. Meanwhile the complexities of the industrial community increased, and the discontents and tensions mounted.

It seems increasingly clear, at least to me, that while some administrative practices and personnel techniques may be better than others, their futility arises from the philosophical assumptions or value judgments on which this superstructure of manipulative procedure rests. We observe again and again that a manager with sound values and a stewardship conception of his role as boss can be a pretty effective leader even though his techniques are quite unorthodox. I am convinced that workers have a fine sensitivity to spiritual qualities and want to work for a boss who believes in something and in whom they can believe.

This observation leads me to suspect that we may have defined the basic purposes and objectives of our industrial enterprise too narrowly, too selfishly, too materialistically. Bread alone will not satisfy workers. There are some indications that our people have lost faith in the basic values of our economic society, and that we need a spiritual rebirth in industrial leadership.

Certainly no people have ever had so much, and enjoyed so little real satisfaction. Our economy has been abundantly productive, our standard of living is at an all-time peak, and yet we are a tense, frustrated, and insecure people full of hostilities and anxieties. Can it be that our *god of production* has feet of clay? Does industry need a new religion—or at least a better one than it has had?

I am convinced that the central problem is not the division of the spoils as organized labor would have us believe. Raising the price of prostitution does not make it the equivalent of love. Is our industrial discontent not in fact the expression of a hunger for a work life that has meaning in terms of higher and more enduring spiritual values? How can we preserve the wholeness of the personality if we are expected to worship God on Sundays and holidays and Mammon on Mondays through Fridays?

I do not imply that this search for real meaning in life is or should be limited to the hours on the job, but I do hold that the central values of our industrial society permeate our entire culture. I am sure we do not require a bill of particulars of the spiritual sickness of our time. The evidences of modern man's search for his soul are all about us. Save for the Communist countries there has been a world-wide revival of interest in religion. The National Council of Churches reports that 62 per cent of our total population, or 103 million, now claim church affiliation.

Perhaps even more significant is the renaissance in the quality of religious thought and experience. Quite evidently our religion of materialism, science, and humanism is not considered adequate. Man is searching for anchors outside himself. He runs wearily to the periphery of the spider web of his own reason and logic, and looks for new "skyhooks"—for an abiding faith around which life's experiences can be integrated and given meaning.

Why "Skyhooks"?

Perhaps we should assume that this need for "skyhooks" is part of man's natural equipment—possibly a function of his intelligence—or if you prefer, God manifesting Himself in His creatures. It seems to me, however, that the recent intensification of this need (or perhaps the clearer recognition of it) stems in part from certain broad social, economic, political, and philosophical trends. I shall not attempt a comprehensive treatment of these, but shall allude to only a few.

Abundance without Satisfaction

I have already indicated that on the economic front we have won the battle of production. We have moved from an economy of scarcity to one of abundance. We have become masters of the physical world and have learned how to convert its natural resources to the satisfaction of our material wants. We are no longer so dependent and so intimately bound to the world of nature. In a way we have lost our feeling of being part of nature and with it our humble reverence for God's creation.

While the industrialization of our economy resulted in ever-increasing production, it also made of individual man a production number—an impersonal, de-skilled, interchangeable production unit, measured in so many cents per hour. For most employees, work no longer promotes the growth of personal character by affording opportunities for personal decision, exercise of judgment, and individual responsibility. An article in *Nation's Business* quotes the modern British philosopher, Alexander Lindsay, on this point as follows:

Industrialism has introduced a new division into society. It is the division between those who manage and take responsibility and those who are managed and have responsibility taken from them. This is a division more important than the division between the rich and poor.[1]

Certainly the modern industrial worker has improved his material standard of living at the cost of becoming more and more dependent on larger and larger groups. Not only his dignity but also his security has suffered. And so he reaches out for new "skyhooks"—for something to believe in, for something that will give meaning to his job.

Disillusionment with Science

A second trend which seems to bear some relation to our urgent need for a faith grows out of our disillusionment with science. As a result of the rapid advance of science, the curtains of ignorance and superstition have been pulled wide on all fronts of human curiosity and knowledge. Many of the bonds of our intellectual enslavement have been broken. Reason and scientific method were called on to witness to the truth, the whole truth, and nothing but the truth. We were freed from the past—its traditions, beliefs, philosophies, its mores, morals, and religion. Science became our religion, and reason replaced emotion.

However, even before the atom bomb there was a growing realization that science did not represent the whole truth, that with all its pretensions it could be dead wrong, and, finally and particularly, that without proper moral safeguards the truth did not necessarily make men free. Atomic fission intensified the fear and insecurity of every one of us who contemplated the possibility of the concentration of power in the hands of men without morals. We want science to be in the hands of men who not only recognize their responsibility to man-made ethical standards (which are easily perverted) but have dedicated themselves to the eternal and abso-

[1] John Kord Lagemann, "Job Enlargement Boosts Production," *Nation's Business,* December 1954, p. 36.

lute standards of God. Thus, while the evidence of material science has been welcomed, our own personal experiences will not permit us to believe that life is merely a whirl of atoms without meaning, purpose, beauty, or destiny.

Trend toward Bigness

A third factor contributing to our insecurity is the trend toward bigness and the resulting loss of individuality. This is the day of bigger and bigger business—in every aspect of life. The small is being swallowed by the big, and the big by the bigger. This applies to business, to unions, to churches, to education, to research and invention, to newspapers, to our practice of the professions, to government, and to nations. Everything is getting bigger except the individual, and he is getting smaller and more insignificant and more dependent on larger social units. Whether we like it or not this is becoming an administrative society, a planned and controlled society, with ever-increasing concentration of power. This is the day of collectivism and public-opinion polls. It is the day when the individual must be *adjusted to the group*—when he must above all else be sensitive to the feelings and attitudes of others, must get an idea of how others expect him to act, and then react to this.

This is the insecure world which David Riesman has described so well in his book, *The Lonely Crowd*.[2] He pictures man as being no longer "tradition-directed" as was primitive man, nor as in colonial days is he "inner-directed" as if by the gyroscope of his own ideals, but today he is "other-directed" as if by radar. He must constantly keep his antenna tuned to the attitudes and reactions of others to him. The shift has been from morals to morale and from self-reliance to dependence on one's peer group. However, the members of one's peer group are each responding to each other. Obviously these shifting sands of public opinion offer no stable values around which life can be consistently integrated and made meaningful. The high-water mark of adjustment in such a society is that the individual be socially accepted and above all else that he appear to be *sincere*.

This is certainly not a favorable environment for the develop-

[2] New Haven, Yale University Press, 1950.

ment of steadfast character. It is essentially a neurotic and schizo-phrenic environment which breeds insecurity.

This socially dependent society also offers an ideal market for the wares of the "huckster," the propagandist, and the demagogue. Lacking a religious interpretation of the divine nature of man, these merchants in mass reaction have sought the least common denominator in human nature and have beamed the movies and newspapers at the ten-year mental level. One wonders if this ap-proach to people does not make them feel that they have been sold short and that they are capable of much better than is expected of them. Has this demoralizing exposure of the cheapness of our values not intensified our search for something better to believe in?

On top of all these disturbing socioeconomic trends came the war. This certainly was materialism, science, and humanism car-ried to the logical conclusion. The war made us question our values and our direction. It left us less cocksure that we were right, and more fearful of ourselves as well as of others. It made us fearful of the power which we had gained, and led us to search our souls to determine whether we had the moral strength to assume the leader-ship role that had been given to us. We have been humbled in our efforts to play God and are about ready to give the job back. Note, however, that this is not a characteristic reaction to war. Typically wars have been followed by a noticeable deterioration of moral standards, traditional values, and social institutions.

Perhaps none of these rationalizations for our return to religion is entirely valid. I suspect that the search for some kind of over-arching integrative principle or idea is the expression of a normal human need. Certainly history would indicate that man's need for a God is eternal even though it may be more keenly sensed in times of adversity. A religion gives a point of philosophical orientation around which life's experiences can be organized and digested. Without the equivalent, a personality cannot be whole and healthy. Short-term goals which need to be shifted with the changing tide do not serve the same integrative function as do the "skyhooks" which are fastened to eternal values. I do not personally regard the current religious revival as a cultural hangover, nor as a regression. Being a mystic I prefer instead to view the need for such a faith as the spark of the Creator in us to drive us on to achieve His will and our own divine destiny.

WHY MONDAY THROUGH FRIDAY?

If we may grant for the moment that modern man *is* searching for deeper meanings in life, we may then ask: What has this to do with industry? If he needs "skyhooks," let him get them in church, or work out his own salvation. The business leaders of the past insisted that "business is business" and that it had little bearing on the individual's private life and philosophy.

There are several reasons why "skyhooks" must be a primary concern of the business administrator:

(1) For the individual the job is the center of life, and its values must be in harmony with the rest of life if he is to be a whole and healthy personality.

(2) This is an industrial society, and its values tend to become those of the entire culture.

(3) The public is insisting that business leaders are in fact responsible for the general social welfare—that the manager's responsibilities go far beyond those of running the business. They have delegated this responsibility to the business executive whether he wishes to play this role or not.

(4) Even if the administrator insists on a narrow definition of his function as merely the production of goods and services as efficiently as possible, it is nevertheless essential that he take these intangibles into account since they are the real secrets of motivating an organization.

(5) Besides all this the administrator needs a better set of "skyhooks" himself if he is to carry his ever-increasing load of responsibility without cracking up. The fact that so many administrators are taking time to rationalize, defend, and justify the private enterprise system is an outward indication of this need for more significant meanings.

ANYTHING WRONG WITH CAPITALISM?

We may ask, then: What specifically is wrong with our capitalistic system of private enterprise? What is wrong with production or with trying to improve our standard of living? What is wrong with a profit, or with private ownership of capital, or with competition? Is this not the true American way of life?[3]

Nothing is necessarily wrong with these values. There are cer-

[3] For a comprehensive treatment of the criticisms of business see J. D. Glover, *The Attack on Big Business* (Boston, Division of Research, Harvard Business School, 1954).

tainly worse motives than the profit motive. A refugee from Communism is reported to have observed: "What a delight to be in the United States where things are produced and sold with such a nice clean motive as making a profit."

I am not an economist. But I am tempted to make a couple of observations about these traditional economic concepts:

1. That while the values represented by them are not necessarily wrong, they are certainly pretty thin and do not challenge the best in people.
2. That many of the classical economic assumptions are outmoded and are no longer adequate descriptions of the actual operation of our present-day economy.

For example, the concept of economic man as being motivated by self-interest not only is outmoded by the best current facts of the social sciences, but also fails to appeal to the true nobility of spirit of which we are capable.

The concept of the free and competitive market is a far cry from the highly controlled and regulated economy in which business must operate today. The typical company does not appear to want to put other companies in the same industry out of business, and in the case of a company hard pressed in the market even the union may decide not to press its economic advantage to the logical conclusion. The assumption that everyone is out to destroy his competitors does not explain the sharing of technology through trade associations and journals. No, we also have tremendous capacity for cooperation when challenged by larger visions. We are daily denying the Darwinian notion of the "survival of the fittest" which, incidentally, William Graham Sumner, one of the nineteenth-century apologists for our economic system, used for justifying unbridled self-interest and competition.

Certainly the traditional concept of private ownership of capital does not quite correspond to the realities of today's control of large blocks of capital by insurance companies and trusteed funds.

The notion of individual security through the accumulation of savings has largely given way to the collectivist means of group insurance, company annuities, and Social Security.

The concept that all profits belong to the stockholders is no longer enthusiastically supported by either the government or the unions, since both are claiming an increasing cut.

And so, while we may argue that the system of private enterprise is self-regulatory and therefore offers maximum individual freedom, the simple, cold fact is that it is in ever-increasing degree a managed or controlled economy—partly at the insistence of the voters, but largely as the result of the inevitable economic pressures and the trend toward bigness.

Regardless of the rightness or wrongness of these changes in our system of enterprise, the changes have been considerable, and I doubt that classical economic theory can be used as an adequate rationale of its virtues. I am therefore not particularly optimistic about the efficacy of the current campaign to have businessmen "save the private-enterprise system and the American way of life" by engaging in wholesale economic education, much of which is based on outmoded concepts.

Much as economic theory needs revision, I fear that this is not likely to cure our ills. Nor do I believe that profit sharing or any other device for increasing the workers' cut (desirable as these efforts may be) will give us what we really want. It is rather another type of sharing that is needed, a sharing of more worthy objectives, a sharing of the management function, and a sharing of mutual respect and Christian working relationships.

Goals and Purposes

What is wrong is more a matter of goals and purposes—of our assumptions about what we are trying to do and how we can dignify and improve ourselves in the doing. There is nothing wrong with production, but we should ask ourselves: *"Production for what?"* Do we use people for production or production for people? How can production be justified if it destroys personality and human values both in the process of its manufacture and by its end use? Clarence B. Randall, former president of Inland Steel Company, in his book, *A Creed for Free Enterprise,* says:

We have come to worship production as an end in itself, which of course it is not. It is precisely there that the honest critic of our way of life makes his attack and finds us vulnerable. Surely there must be for each person some ultimate value, some purpose, some mode of self-expression that makes the experience we call life richer and deeper.[4]

So far, so good, Mr. Randall. But now notice how he visualizes industry making its contribution to this worthy objective:

To produce more and more with less and less effort is merely treading water unless we *thereby release time and energy for the cultivation of the mind and the spirit* and for the achievement of those ends for which Providence placed us on this earth.[5]

Here is the same old dichotomy—work faster and more efficiently so that you can finish your day of drudgery and cultivate your soul on your own time. In fact he says: "A horse with a very evil disposition can nevertheless pull the farmer's plow." No, I am afraid the job *is* the life. *This* is what must be made meaningful. We cannot assume that the end of production justifies the means. What happens to people in the course of producing may be far more important than the end product. Materialism is not a satisfactory "skyhook." People are capable of better and want to do better. (Incidentally I have the impression that Randall's practices line up well with my own point of view even if his words do not.)

Perhaps we should ask what is the really important difference between Russian Communism and our system. Both worship production and are determined to produce more efficiently, and do. Both worship science. Both have tremendously improved the standard of living of their people. Both share the wealth. Both develop considerable loyalties for their system. (In a mere forty years since Lenin started the Communist revolution a third of the world's people have come to accept its allegiance.) True, in Russia capital is controlled by the state while here it is theoretically controlled by individuals, although in actual practice, through absentee ownership, it is controlled to a considerable extent by central planning agencies and bureaus, both public and private.

No, the real difference is in the philosophy about people and how they may be used as means to ends. It is a difference in the assumptions made about the origin of rights—whether the individual is endowed with rights by his Creator and yields these only

[4] Boston, Little, Brown and Company, 1952, p. 16.
[5] *Ibid.*

voluntarily to civil authority designated by him, or whether rights originate in force and in the will of the government. Is God a myth, or is He the final and absolute judge to whom we are ultimately responsible? Are all standards of conduct merely man-made and relative, or absolute and eternal? Is man a meaningless happenstance of protoplasm, or is he a divine creation with a purpose, with potential for improvement, and with a special destiny in the over-all scheme of things?

These are some of the differences—or at least I hope that they still are. And what a difference these intangible, perhaps mythical, "skyhooks" make. They are nevertheless the most real and worthwhile and enduring things in the world. The absence of these values permitted the Nazis to "process" people through the gas chambers in order to recover the gold in their teeth.

The Administrator Contributes

This, then, is part of our general cultural heritage and is passed on to us in many ways. However, it really comes to life in people—in their attitudes, aspirations, and behaviors. And in a managerial society this brings us back to the quality of the individual administrator. He interprets or crystallizes the values and objectives for his group. He sets the climate within which these values either *do* or *do not* become working realities. He must define the goals and purposes of his group in larger and more meaningful perspective. He integrates the smaller, selfish goals of individuals into larger, more social and spiritual objectives for the group. He provides the vision without which the people perish. Conflicts are resolved by relating the immediate to the long-range and more enduring values. In fact, we might say this *integrative function* is the core of the administrator's contribution.

The good ones have the mental equipment to understand the business and set sound long-term objectives, but the best ones have in addition the philosophical and character values which help them to relate the over-all goals of the enterprise to eternal values. This is precisely the point at which deep-seated religious convictions can serve an integrative function, since they represent the most long-range of all possible goals. Most really great leaders in all fields of human endeavor have been peculiarly sensitive to their historic role in human destiny. Their responsibility and loyalty are to some distant vision which gives calm perspective to the hot issues of the day.

This function of the administrator goes far beyond being a likable personality, or applying correct principles of organization, or being skillful in the so-called techniques of human relations. I am convinced that the difficulties which so many executives have with supervisory relationships cannot be remedied by cultivation of the so-called human relations skills. These difficulties spring rather from one's conception of his function or role as a boss, his notion about the origin and nature of his authority over others, the assumptions he makes about people and their worth, and his view of what he and his people are trying to accomplish together. To illustrate:

If, for example, my personal goal is to get ahead in terms of money, position, and power; and if I assume that to achieve this I must best my competitors; that the way to do this is to establish a good production record; that my employees are means to this end; that they are replaceable production units which must be skillfully manipulated; that this can be done by appealing to the lowest form of immediate selfish interest; that the greatest threat to me is that my employees may not fully recognize my authority nor accept my leadership—if these are my values, then I am headed for trouble, all supervisory techniques notwithstanding.

I wish I could be so positive in painting the picture of the right values and approaches to management. I suspect there are many, many different right answers. No doubt each company or enterprise will have to define its own long-term purposes and develop its own philosophy in terms of its history, traditions, and its real function in our economy. I am also certain that no one philosophy would be equally useful to all managers. The character of an organization is, to a large extent, set by the top man or the top group, and it is inevitable that this be the reflection of the philosophy of these individuals. No one of us can operate with another's philosophy. I have also observed that in most enterprises the basic faith or spirit of the organization is a rather nebulous or undefined something, which nevertheless has very profound meaning to the employees.

A Successful Executive

Recognizing, then, the futility of advocating any one pattern of values, it occurs to me that it might, however, be suggestive or helpful if I told you something of the philosophy of one extremely successful executive whom I have pumped a good deal on this subject (for he is more inclined to live his values than to talk about them):

As near as I can piece it together, he believes that this world was not an accident but was created by God, that His laws regulate and control the universe, and that we are ultimately *responsible to Him*. Man, as God's supreme creation, is in turn endowed with creative ability. Each individual represents a unique combination of talents and potentials. In addition, man is the only animal endowed with freedom of choice and with a high capacity for making value judgments. With these gifts (of heredity and cultural environment) goes an obligation to give the best possible accounting of one's stewardship in terms of maximum self-development and useful service to one's fellows in the hope that one may live a rich life and be a credit to one's Creator.

This executive also assumes that each individual possesses certain God-given rights of self-direction which only *the individual* can voluntarily delegate to others in authority over him, and that this is usually done in the interest of achieving some mutual cooperative good. The executive therefore assumes that his *own* authority as boss over others must be exercised with due regard for the attendant obligations to his employees and to the stockholders who have temporarily and voluntarily yielded their rights in the interest of this common undertaking. (Notice that he does not view his authority as originating with or derived from his immediate superior.) This delegated authority must, of course, be used to advance the common good rather than primarily to achieve the selfish ambitions of the leader at the expense of the led.

He further assumes that the voluntary association of employees in industry is for the purpose of increasing the creativity and productivity of all members of the group and thus of bringing about increased benefits to all who may share in the ultimate use of these goods and services. What is equally important, however, is that in the course of this industrial operation each individual should have an opportunity to develop the maximum potential of his skills and that the working relationships should not destroy the individual's ability to achieve his greatest maturity and richness of experience. As supervisor he must set the working conditions and atmosphere which will make it possible for his employees to achieve this dual objective of increasing productivity and maximizing self-development.

These goals can best be achieved by giving employees maximum opportunity to exercise their capacity for decision making and judgment within their assigned area of responsibility. The supervisor is then primarily a coach who must instruct, discipline, and motivate all the members of the group, making it possible for each to exercise his special talent in order to maximize the total team contribution. Profits are regarded as a measure of the group's progress toward these goals, and a loss represents not only an improper but even an immoral use of the talents of the group.

There is nothing "soft" about his operation. He sets high quality standards and welcomes stiff competition as an additional challenge to his group. He therefore expects and gets complete cooperation and dedication on the part of everyone. Incidentally, he views the activity of working together in this manner with others as being one of life's most rewarding experiences. He holds that this way of life is something which we have not yet fully learned, but that its achievement is part of our divine destiny. He is firmly convinced that such conscientious efforts *will* be rewarded with success. He manages with a light touch that releases creativity, yet with complete confidence in the outcome.

This is probably a poor attempt at verbalizing the basic philosophy which this man lives so easily and naturally. I hope, however, that it has revealed something of his conception of his role or function as an executive, and his view of what he and his organization are trying to do together. With this account of his values I am sure that you would have no difficulty completing the description of his administrative practices and operating results. They flow naturally from his underlying faith, without benefit of intensive training in the principles and art of administration.

As you would suspect, people like to work for him—or with him. He attracts good talent (which is one of the real secrets of success). Those with shoddy values, selfish ambitions, or character defects do not survive—the organization is self-pruning. Those who remain develop rapidly because they learn to accept responsibility. He not only advocates but practices decentralization and delegation. His employees will admit that they have made mistakes, but usually add with a grin that they try not to make the same one twice. People respond to his leadership because he has faith in them and expects the best in them rather than the worst. He speaks well of the members of his organization, and they appear to be proud of each other and of their record of performance. He takes a keen interest in developing measurements of performance and in better-ing previous records or competitive standards. He feels that no one has a right to "louse up a job"—a point on which he feels the stockholders and the Lord are in complete agreement.

While he does not talk much about "employee communications" nor stress formal programs of this type, his practice is to spend a large proportion of his time in the field with his operating people rather than in his office. He is "people-oriented" and does a particularly good job of listening. The union committee members have confidence in his fairness, yet do a workmanlike job of bargaining. In administering salaries he seems to be concerned about helping the individual to improve his contribution so that a pay increase can be justified.

In his general behavior he moves without haste or hysteria. He is typically well organized, relaxed, and confident, even under trying circumstances. There is a high degree of consistency in his behavior and in the quality of his decisions because his basic values do not shift. Since he does not operate by expediency, others can depend on him; and this consistency makes for efficiency in the discharge of delegated responsibility. Those operating problems which do come to him for decision seem to move easily and quickly to a conclusion. His long-term values naturally express themselves in well-defined policies, and it is against this frame of reference that the decisions of the moment easily fall into proper perspective.

In policy-level discussions his contributions have a natural quality of objectivity because "self-concern" does not confuse. Others take him at face value because his motives are not suspect. When differences or conflicts do arise, his approach is not that of compromise; rather he attempts to integrate the partisan views around mutually acceptable longer-range goals. The issues of the moment then seem to dissolve in a discussion of the best means to the achievement of the objective. I have no doubt that he also has some serious problems, but I have tried to give a faithful account of the impression which he creates. There is a *sense of special significance* about his operation which is shared by his associates.

THIS IS THE KEY

It is precisely this "sense of special significance" which is the key to leadership. We all know that there are many different ways of running a successful operation. I am certainly not recommending any particular set of administrative practices—although admittedly some are better than others. Nor am I suggesting that his set of values should be adopted by others, or for that matter could be. What I am saying is that a man's real values have a subtle but inevitable way of being communicated, and they affect the significance of everything he does.

These are the vague intangibles—the "skyhooks"—which are difficult to verbalize but easy to sense and tremendously potent in their influence. They provide a different, invisible, fundamental structure into which the experiences of every day are absorbed and given meaning. They are frequently unverbalized, and in many organizations they defy definition. Yet they are the most real things in the world.

The late Jacob D. Cox, Jr., formerly president of Cleveland Twist Drill Company, told a story that illustrates my point:

Jimmy Green was a new union committee member who stopped in to see Mr. Cox after contract negotiations had been concluded. Jimmy said that every other place he had worked, he had always gone home grouchy; he never wanted to play with the children or take his wife to the movies. And then he said, "But since I have been working here, all that has changed. Now when I come home, the children run to meet me and we have a grand romp together. It is a wonderful difference and I don't know why, but I thought you would like to know."[6]

As Cox observed, there must be a lot of Jimmy Greens in the world who want an opportunity to take part freely in a cooperative effort that has a moral purpose.

LETTERS OF COMMENT

Mr. Ohmann and the Editors of the *Harvard Business Review* have received hundreds of letters of comment. Some of them have been enthusiastic, some critical, but the response has been overwhelmingly favorable. The letters which follow are selected to illustrate different points of view.

FROM:

R. S. Owen, Senior Partner

R. S. Owen & Company

[6] *Material Human Progress* (Cleveland, Cleveland Twist Drill Company, 1954), p. 104.

Mr. Ohmann opens up an avenue of thinking that makes interesting walking, and I would like to accept this challenge to walk with him for at least one thought.

A few years back I brought together several men (heads of their businesses), each of whom wanted to improve his own production by exchanging know-how and experience. This was to be carried out by their production supervisors in subsequent clinics and monthly exchange of production and cost information.

During our first luncheon together there was the customary patter of exploratory talk; many were meeting for the first time. Someone mentioned an incident in his church, and it developed that every man in the room held a position of responsibility in a church. The companies represented were small companies, all in the same business. I thought at the time that it augured well for the success of a venture which is dependent on a high degree of individual honesty and integrity that these men had accepted responsibilities in their churches and lived their lives accordingly.

As I have come to know this group of men better, I have observed a similar pattern of administrative behavior. This becomes most apparent in matters that concern people—there is always a calm consideration of all the aspects of any given situation. Also, as I have come to know the personnel within these various companies, I find an unusually high degree of loyalty to the company's interests and the bossman.

Another experience of the past two years that bears on the subject concerns the field of wage incentives. In the particular industry in which we operate, wage incentive systems have had a varied record. It is my business to install such arrangements. In several instances recently I have urged that production standards be established and allowed to run for some time before the impact of the financial incentive is injected. There are several reasons for this, but the primary one is that leadership from the personal interest of supervisors is of such importance to the success of a management plan that, painful though it is, the production improvement should start to come through the leadership medium rather than through the prospect of increase in direct pay. The financial incentive can come later. Leadership that is motivated by personal interest in the other fellow is natural among supervisors who have the stewardship concept.

From these experiences and others, I have a thought to offer along the lines of Mr. Ohmann's article. I submit that a man, particularly in management, is only in his best position to exercise judgment when he himself is feeling his best, things are fine at home, his garden is in good

shape, his opportunities for service in the church and community have
been accepted, the bird house is in good repair and filled with seed, and
his roses are properly pruned and fertilized. In other words, when a man
is in tune with all the things that are God's, he is in tune with God,
and when he is in tune with God, he is in the best possible position to
handle a situation involving people.

FROM:
John Rhodes, Vice President
Interstate Wells

On finishing "Skyhooks," I was convinced Mr. Ohmann was either a
minister or a professor. Turning to the biographical sketch, I was surprised
to find that he had been an industrial relations manager and is now assistant to the president of an oil company. Possibly he entered business on
a high enough level to have escaped a good deal of what I have observed.

I do not know Mr. Ohmann's complete background, but I suspect it
diverges vastly from mine. I went to work at fourteen, and in succession
was delivery boy, stock clerk, office boy, laborer, truck driver, stenog-
rapher, personnel clerk, a series of other positions, and ultimately industrial relations manager. College was a night affair, with the day's
work dominating my existence. I came to know the working staff
thoroughly from laborer through clerk on through section heads, department managers, plant superintendents, staff people, and line people.
And I have reached some vastly different conclusions from Mr. Ohmann's,
probably because of that background.

Before going into these, I hasten to agree with certain points. A
manager with sound values can be effective though unorthodox. People
do need satisfaction for spiritual cravings in the work scene. Man should
be more than a beast. There should be a sharing of management function, mutual respect, and Christian working relationships. I cannot too
strongly *emphasize* the profoundly spiritual side of my own character
which seems to match Mr. Ohmann's. Emphasize, because what follows
may seem to deny it. But it is not a question of what I feel. It's what I
find.

And what I find is an industrial economy which should be the despair
of any deep thinker. Its broad base is populated by all kinds of people,
uneducated and educated, but essentially good and kind. But as soon
as you rise above the lowest levels, you begin to see why Jesus taught
resignation and humility rather than ambition. Ambition turns these
ordinary, kindly people into something almost unnatural. For from the
first supervisory levels to the top, industry is shot through with monsters

who do not know they are evil, who through indifference, neglect, or deliberate intention perpetrate cruelties that are the more horrible because undramatic.

There is no disemboweling of men or stretching them on a rack. That would be preferable, for then the perpetrators would have to face the concrete evidence of what they were doing. But there is a stifling of ambition where it is found, a denial of participation, a lack of natural love and affection, a thwarting of brotherhood, a suppression of creativity, a general attitude which says, "Do just what you're told; take your pay and go home." Any attempt at a warm and full relationship is stiff-armed away by suspicion, greed, and envy.

It is no happenstance that people turn to their churches, their fraternal organizations, and their hobbies for outlets for creative instincts and spiritual communion. The flight to the suburbs, with its concomitant do-it-yourself craftsmanship, is partially the result of personal inability to fulfill oneself in the business field. Managers wistfully wish that they could engender the same fine craftsmanship, the meticulous attention to detail, the fierce concentration, the love, if you will, of the man in his home building a barbecue pit. This they could do, for the man is often putting into his home activities an ardor which has been coldly rejected by industry.

In the plant, he has no sense of belonging, no identification; and all the supervisors, from foreman to superintendent, concert to prevent this sense. They are too busy manifesting their own personalities, protecting their own positions, or destroying that of another to care what happens to the *espirit de corps* of the worker. Abstractly they intensely desire it, on the one hand, and concretely crush it, on the other.

And even where there are top executives like Clarence Randall, men of good will who sincerely want to do the right thing, they are thwarted, first, by not knowing quite how to go about it, and, second, by the impassivity of the great supervisory mass. There may be kindliness above, but right down the line there is indifference, jealousy, and downright cruelty. There are men of tiny stature, who will never take thought to add one cubit.

This is where Mr. Ohmann and I differ. It is my finding that there are so many men consciously or unconsciously evil in the supervisory ranks that nothing can be done about them; and Mr. Ohmann will go to his grave, and I to mine, without any real change in this picture.

Maybe I should not say evil. Say rather that they are psychoneurotic, psychotic, unhappy, frustrated, disturbed. We should feel sorry for them. But the misery they cause by what they do—or do not do—adds up to a staggering total of evil, all of it unnecessary.

And also we should not say, perhaps, that nothing can be done. Psychiatrists could find out why they are overly ambitious, fearful, petty, jealous, and spiteful, and abate their symptoms. But only in theory, since they outnumber the psychiatrists available for their treatment hundreds of times over.

My advice to Mr. Ohmann is to do what good he can in industry, but never expect the millennium of the kindly, competent supervisor and the consequently happy, fulfilled employee. Experience is against it.

FROM:
Wallace C. Speers, Vice President
James McCutcheon & Co.[7]

My only hesitation on complete agreement with Mr. Ohmann comes from experience. The spiritual factor or nonphysical love or whatever you want to call it is not soft or sanctimonius, nor is it just sweetness and light. Christ himself said again and again that "the law must be fulfilled." I take that to mean economic law or any part of the natural law.

The danger in approaching the reaching out for the spiritual factor in terms of everyday life comes from the false conception that it *replaces* everything. It doesn't. It *conditions* everything.

The result is that if a cleric approaches this idea without direct personal experience and appreciation of the hard knocks of real life, he is in danger of ending up with something that may be wishy-washy at best or pink at worst.

Even if an experienced businessman approaches it with the idea that the spiritual factor replaces energy, efficiency, skill, imagination, or ability, he will fall flat on his face in terms of economics.

The best hope of success is a hard-boiled businessman who is eminently successful at getting a vision of the place the spiritual factor must play in business and letting it condition his approach to every phase of it without letting it affect any of the economic or natural laws in his operation.

I have almost ruined a department and perhaps more than one man by trying to substitute kindness for discipline and the natural strict requirements of method.

The best example of what I mean is contained in an experience of mine. In doing an act of kindness by taking an elderly lady home late at night, I turned too sharply into her driveway and crumpled my fender on a retaining wall. No matter how wonderful the motivation or how good the deed, God does not withdraw His natural laws.

[7] Mr. Speers is chairman of The Laymen's Movement for a Christian World.

Skill, ability, experience, imagination, and so forth still have to be maintained; otherwise the spiritual factor loses its effectiveness entirely. That does not deny its critically important central position in everyday life if we are to find satisfaction or provide a workable pattern. It merely points out the setting in which it must be used.

FROM:

Walter H. Rupp, Technical Adviser
Esso Research and Engineering Company

I would like to try adding a few thoughts and perhaps a suggested refinement to "Skyhooks."

Factually, individuals in the United States are turning toward God increasingly. Some embrace Him; some merely glance His way. There is great comfort for all men in God's Church, and if it is possible for us only to worship on Sundays, that is a start. But what of Monday through Friday (and Saturday too)? Where are these individuals then?

Are not the "Sunday individuals" being "teamized" on Monday through Friday, and sometimes on Saturday too? "Teamized" by being led into paths where the robe of individualism is tattered and the tent of group action rises to shelter the faceless people comprising the "team." In return for this loss of individuality, we have achieved a higher standard of material living (sometimes even a higher standard than we need or want). The "Abundance without Satisfaction" result that Ohmann discussed is our lot five-sevenths or six-sevenths of the time.

And why should this be? Of course I don't know "why." I can only tell how a few individuals seem to feel about it. Industrial living often has failed to supply *life* to its members. Rather it tends to sap the individual's will and asks him to abdicate in favor of a fictitious being—a "corporation." And in return for work and loyalty, he receives material possessions—pensions, group insurance, Social Security, and discounts on company products.

How can we bring the five-sevenths or six-sevenths of the week closer to the Sunday one-seventh? Can business and love of the individual be made compatible? I think they can. With frank admission of oversimplification, I'm sure that love can be practiced in everyday business life. Now the definition of "business love" is far different from "love" as used on Sunday and in our family circles. The English language has room for many words denoting love of different kinds. Other languages often have five or six words describing love of different degrees and applications.

By "business love" is meant the desire to help other people up the ladder, to rehabilitate workers who have some blind spots in talent or personality, to show concern for feelings ahead of the dollar sign, to think more of some individual's progress than maybe even he himself thinks of it, and finally to look beyond the daily job and find a true meaning in our industrial life as one of God's necessary operations for human welfare. In other words, our daily work is a means of sustaining life to be used for His improvement of all humanity.

This expression is not as clear as crystal. But in my own mind, it is crystal clear that if those of us in business will look at each individual man as what he *might be,* then the spirit of God's hope will be with us seven-sevenths of the time. In my personal view, this is "business love." It can give meaning to business life.

FROM:
Esther I. Persson
Editorial Staff, *Banking*

The uneasy feeling I have had ever since reading "Skyhooks" is like the old jingle:

> "I do not like thee, Dr. Fell;
> The reason why I cannot tell."

Partly for my own peace of mind, and partly because of the author's disarming invitation, I have tried to analyze and to set down the reasons for my vague dislike and fear of the ideology implied in the article.

First, the underlying philosophy has an unpleasant familiarity. Where have I met its counterparts? In the theories of Communism, Fascism, and Nazism. Does this sound shocking? Perhaps. But when an attempt is made to equate a philosophy of life with a philosophy of industrial production, the result looks much like Mussolini's corporate state, in which a man works in conformity with the philosophy of his economic master. All forms of thought control and brainwashing—whether actuated by good or evil intent—are repulsive.

This particular brand of thought control is perhaps more repellent than the Communist variety, because it masquerades under the guise of goodness, and offers itself as a counteroffensive to Communism. But opposing one evil with another, more subtle, evil will not cure or improve whatever ails the Western industrial world.

Second, Mr. Ohmann expresses opinions as if they were facts. He has a right to believe, for example, that "no people have ever had so much, and enjoyed so little real satisfaction. . . . We are a tense, frustrated, and insecure people full of hostilities and anxieties." That's one man's opinion, but I don't agree with it. Of course all adults have worries, but that does not make us a nation of neurotics. When in the history of the human race has man not had worries and even frustrations?

The so-called revival of interest in religion may only be a search for social conformity. Whether or not a business or industrial executive goes to church does not affect his talent to get along with subordinates and peers, his creative and imaginative understanding of others, or any other admirable quality of character.

We look with amusement on the smug conformity of the Victorians, and we admire men like Darwin and Huxley who let in a breath of fresh air. They, too, were mystics, although not in the Victorian sense. And now again it looks as if the only people who are "mystics" are those who conform to a specific ritual way of life. We are fairly well along to becoming smug Victorians. No one had a deeper feeling of being part of nature than men like Darwin. How can we define "God" and "God's creation"? And if each one of us *could* adequately define these terms, we would find as many definitions as definers—and who would presume to affix the *imprimatur* on the ultimate "correct" definition?

"For the individual the job is the center of life." This, too, is opinion, not fact. For the vast majority of persons who depend on their jobs, the getting, and the keeping, and the bettering of their jobs is important *economically,* but surely their job is not the center of life.

And, finally, I am glad I do not have to work either for or with the "extremely successful executive" whose portrait the author draws in such detail. Of course such an organization is "self-pruning" just as any thought-controlled organization must be. For my own part, I'd rather work for Clarence Randall.

FROM:

Claude Robinson, President
Opinion Research Corporation

"Skyhooks" is an indication of some of the mental stirrings that are currently going on in industry.

Here we have long been impressed by the research evidence that says that man does not live by bread alone and the motivational power of what we call the nonfinancial reward, or reward of the spirit. We have not undertaken to link our philosophy to a religious system, for obvious reasons, but we are quite conscious of the values that are being discussed.

A year ago I had the pleasure of spending a week walking up and down the beach with an Episcopal bishop discussing all manner of affairs, including problems of industry. I was quite struck by the fact that we came to many of the same conclusions—he by the theological route and I by the research route.

As a matter of fact, we think we note an increasing interest in the whole area of nonfinancial job values. More companies such as Du Pont, Standard Oil Company of New Jersey, and others, for example, are giving thought to this subject in practical terms.

One specific point: the article appears to argue that the trend toward bigness is incompatible with individuality. When I was doing graduate work in sociology, we used to talk a good deal about this issue; and I am inclined to believe that what the sociologists call "primary group controls" are more tyrannical in small population units than in large population units. In a big city there is possibly a greater diversification of labor and therefore more opportunity for individuals to exercise their individuality. If you desire to ride your bicycle down a street on a moonlit night, you can possibly find other people in a big city who desire to do likewise; but in a smaller community you are only subject to ridicule.

FROM:

E. L. Quirin, Director of Research
Babson's Reports, Inc.

Most of the following thoughts are only nuances, but important ones, I believe. Assuredly my views pertain to perhaps only one per cent of "Skyhooks." As for the rest, I say "Amen!"

Naturally, we all hope for the best from the notable revival of attendance and sincere participation in religious services. However, I am inclined to wonder whether *so far* this may have meant more a bonanza for the churches as organizations than an awakening to spiritual freedom for the individual. The "disillusionment with science" should not go so far as to cause us to forget the "many bonds of our intellectual enslavement which it has broken" and to drive us back to the peaceful drug of orthodoxy's false authority which still proclaims its right to enslave minds for the promise of rewards. Let us not endanger stifling the seed of honest introspection, such as "Skyhooks," by placing it among the same weeds, or in the same pasture, as the dogmatically intolerant castes which are still the most tempting refuge to the lost soul.

In other words, I do believe in encouraging introspection and the seeking of spiritually healthy truths and codes of behavior, which one associates with "going to church," but I believe today's world requires that one go to church with a questioning mind, and not an obediently blind one which is demanded of some adherents. This may seem trite. Yet we must not overlook the fact that lost souls will grab at any seeming hope. Politically lost, Germany followed Hitler. Should our religion-lost people follow the church that promises most in its humble-seeming, self-appointed role (whichever religion it may be among the many in that category)? Should we not question whether our organized religions are in harmony with present-day life? Are they really the spiritual conveyance they claim to be?

Elsewhere Mr. Ohmann mentions that in Russia capital is controlled by the state and that everywhere capital is controlled by bureaus and agencies, public or private. It seems to me that the world has been suffering for several centuries now from the frustration caused by overlooking the fact that a state, a bureau, a corporation, all are individuals. We should all forever be aware that such legal concepts do not alter nature. I do not believe that the United States exists in God's view of world responsibilities, or, in that sense, the corporation I work for. These are inventions of the mind—like clubs, churches, political parties. So regardless of the artifice "legal ownership," such as the state, the corporation, the churches, only individuals must be recognized as the owners through, and under the terms of, the organization which they, the controlling individuals, operate.

FROM:

Kermit Fischer, President
Fischer and Porter Company

"Skyhooks" gave me much encouragement and nourishment. I think the five reasons Mr. Ohmann has given why "skyhooks" must be a primary concern of the business administrator are particularly valuable and give me much gratification because they express so lucidly thoughts which I have at various times tried to convey without too much success to other industrial executives.

While we have emerged from the "beat them over the back" stage of industrial exploitation, we have as yet only graduated into the "optimum carrot determination" stage. Our industrial managers do "feed" the workers instead of "beating" them, but the main effort seems to be directed toward determining the optimum length and diameter of the carrot which shall be dangled in front of the worker and the optimum interval at which he shall be permitted to have a nibble. Granted, the carrot is getting bigger and longer every year. And, furthermore, the worker is taking ever larger bites out of the carrot. However, there seems to be too little recognition among the management class that "business leaders are in fact responsible for the general social welfare" and that it is their obligation to see that their employees have the greatest opportunity for health, happiness, security, and the full realization of their latent capacities.

FROM:
Rev. Charles B. Aziere, O.S.B., Editor
Catholic Business Education Review[8]

We were agreeably surprised by "Skyhooks": first, because there is so much Catholic philosophy of business in it; secondly, because we found it in the *Harvard Business Review*. We are not going to challenge Mr. Ohmann's thinking, for we agree with most of it, but we are going to suggest some further refinement.

What we would like to refine in Mr. Ohmann's thinking is the "why" of his philosophy, or the lack of a philosophy, since he doesn't seem to be very sure of himself in this portion of his article. We are not going to be quite as positive as Mr. Ohmann that "no one philosophy would be equally useful to all managers," but we hope to show why we *believe* that one is.

We do believe there is one philosophy equally useful to all managers —the philosophy of Jesus Christ. And we believe that all managers *can* operate in accordance with this philosophy, especially if they will accept the interpretation of St. Thomas Aquinas, as correlated to the philosophy of Aristotle. We believe Mr. Ohmann and some of his readers might be very much surprised at the *one* right answer, as applied to our times, which can be found in the social teachings of Popes Leo XIII, Pius XI, and Pius XII. For a starting point in the refinement of his views, we would recommend to Mr. Ohmann and his readers *The Church Speaks to the Modern World* by Etienne Gilson.

Now the fact that we believe there is one right answer, and Mr. Ohmann believes there are many, many right answers, isn't the basic question. The basic question is this: *On what authority?* If there are many, many right answers, and if each individual is privileged to interpret basic values as he finds them useful to himself or his kind of society, by what right or value basis can he judge Karl Marx, Adam Smith, François Quesnay? Or Descartes, Hegel, or Spencer? Or Lenin, Hitler, or Jefferson? Or Martin Luther, John Wesley, or Leo XIII? Or, for that matter, A Successful Executive? We purposely limit these questions to leaders of Western (Christian?) civilization, because we interpret Mr. Ohmann's views on God as applying to the God of Christianity.

[8] This comment is based on an editorial written by Father Aziere and published in the *Catholic Business Education Review* of June 1955.

We believe the question of authority is the heart of the matter of the "why" of Mr. Ohmann's philosophy. We recognize, also, that this is contrary to Protestantism's basic precept—namely, that every individual can interpret basic values, that there can be many, many different right answers. But if this were true, we could never quite see why the right would not be granted to Karl Marx or Adolf Hitler as well as to Martin Luther and John Wesley. What makes one less free than another to interpret basic values, if all are equally free? We doubt that enough leaders of the Western civilization of our times are yet ready to accept a Supreme Court in the economic and social spheres, as they have long since accepted one in the political field. They will continue to grope for the right answer because they are not ready to go to the source where the right answer will be found.

Yet we like the trend of thinking exemplified by Mr. Ohmann and many others in recent years. It offers a definite movement of reversal of the trend set in motion by the Protestant Reformation. The reformers first denied the *authority* of the Church founded by Jesus Christ. In a later age the rationalists and illuminati denied the *authority* of Christ Himself. It was but a further development for many scientists and social thinkers to deny the *authority* of God as well. The crisis of our age has forced men to take sides on the existence and authority of God. Perhaps this is but a trend of reversal and return to one fold and One Shepherd. At least we may hope that the groping for some kind of unity among those separated from the Catholic Church, the evident attempts at spiritual revival, and the search for a satisfactory theology among Protestant churches will at least lead mankind back to Jesus Christ in our Western society.

FROM:

J. M. Barker, Chairman, Board of Directors
Allstate Insurance Company

I disagree with what Mr. Ohmann says in spots, but that does not mean that I am critical of what he says. For instance, at the bottom of the first page, "Certainly no people have ever had so much and enjoyed so little real satisfaction." That is a pretty broad statement. It is the common coin of present-day comment about Americans in general, but I do not agree with it. I have no real basis for comparison, even though I have been a student of history for many years. Perhaps it is because I do not know how to measure "real satisfaction."

If he is saying that real satisfaction does not stem from material well-being alone, I agree. I consider that the great problem of our civilization is: How do we withstand the ravages of prosperity? I am one of those who think that evolution is a very slow process and that it takes many thousands of years to change man's nature perceptibly. What Mr. Ohmann calls the search for "skyhooks" has characterized man throughout his whole history. We know more about the dissatisfactions of present-day man than we do about the dissatisfactions of the past, because our system of communication is better. Dissatisfaction is one of the penalties of living in an evolutionary world. The stage settings may be different in different ages, but the human elements seem to me to be unchanged. As Karr, the old Frenchman, said, *"Plus ça change, plus c'est la même chose."*

I think Mr. Ohmann is too severe on William Graham Sumner, whom he calls a nineteenth-century apologist for our economic system. Actually Sumner lived from 1840 to 1910, and was the rector of an Episcopal church in Morristown, New Jersey, until 1872, when he went to Yale as a professor of economics. The book Mr. Ohmann probably has in mind is *What Social Classes Owe to Each Other,* published in 1882. In it Sumner made the famous statement that A and B got together and decided what C should do for D. C, the fellow who bore the burden, was the one he called "the forgotten man." Franklin D. Roosevelt twisted Sumner's presentation so that D became the forgotten man, which was good politics and quite in line with the Rooseveltian ideals.

I am inclined to differ, also, in the examination of "the really important difference between Russian Communism and our system." Has Communism in Russia "tremendously improved the standard of living of their people"? I wish that he had defined what the term "Communism" means as practiced in Russia. I do not agree with the statement that "here [capital] is theoretically controlled by individuals, although in actual practice, through absentee ownership, it is controlled to a considerable extent by central planning agencies and bureaus, both public and private." Suppose I have some capital invested in the Standard Oil Company of Ohio. I certainly cannot dictate the company's use of capital, and in that narrow sense I have lost control of the capital. When, however, at a moment's notice I can sell my shares in a public market and get cash for them and use the capital for some other purpose, I maintain that I have a considerable degree of control. I admit freely that I have lost control of the capital which I turn over to the government in tax payments.

I agree with Mr. Ohmann that "the character of an organization is, to a large extent, set by the top man or the top group, and it is inevitable that this be the reflection of the philosophy of these individuals." I should be tempted to make the statement even more emphatic.

The great Egyptologist and philosopher, James H. Breasted, wrote a great book a good many years ago called *The Dawn of Conscience*. In it he showed by translations from the pyramid inscriptions the first faint appearance of what we call conscience in human affairs. In other words, he put his finger on that point in history when historical man in the saddle first accepted some responsibilities for the welfare of the man on the ground. That appears to be the first recorded instance of man accepting any responsibility as his brother's keeper. As time goes on, man has accepted more and more responsibility for his fellow man. Again, an evolutionary process. I have lived a long and active life, and I should say that in it I have seen more progress along that line in this country than has previously taken place over the ages in the world.

Perhaps the most pointed difference of opinion I have is that it does not seem to me that Mr. Ohmann has thought through the implications of the vastly increased world population of a century or two or three hence. In an overpopulated world, all our ideals of the golden rule, the fellowship of man, honesty, decency, and kindliness are bound to go by the board when there are just too many people for the means of subsistence. Let the scientists say that they can take care of the problem by feeding people proteins grown from algae and such stuff. Sooner or later the geometric increase of population is going to catch up with the means of subsistence. I do not mean to be unfair in bringing up this point, but I wish that Mr. Ohmann had looked farther into the future and examined the implications of the continued denial of the principle of the survival of the fittest.

FROM:

J. C. Tugman, Application Engineering
General Electric Company

Mr. Ohmann declares that the enterprise system is so negligent about its impact on the human spirit that its expanding drive puts the whole economic institution on dangerous tension by weakening the foundations of the social structure and developing a new type of individual whose loyalty to the system largely depends on what he can get from it. Mr. Ohmann says that our society is really very sick.

How far we have drifted from the outlook of the colonial pioneers who regarded the primary purpose of their industry as a discipline to develop them for divine favor! It is not hard to see how succeeding generations confused the enriching fruits of the discipline with the divine favor. It is not hard either to understand how their present heirs have built up a magnificent but narrowly conceived institution to produce the fruits on a fabulous scale. It is no wonder we have shifted our reverence from the Lord to the system of production. In the only nation so overfed that weight reduction is systematically advocated, we have yet to awaken to the fact that the life we lead stifles us in our most significant need. We habitually cost-account our activities and interests. We have taken over the logic of production as the guide to what is good for us.

The events in our cultural development which have led us to our present situation are related in Reinhold Niebuhr's *The Irony of American History*. Long ago, he relates, we began to identify prosperity with virtue. He points out that "from the later Puritans to the present day, we have variously attributed American prosperity to our superior diligence, our greater skill or (more presently) to our more fervent devotion to the ideals of freedom." Niebuhr quotes De Tocqueville who said of American preachers of 1835 that "it is often difficult to ascertain from their discourses whether the principal object of religion is to obtain eternal felicity or prosperity in this world."

"Skyhooks" discusses some of the more damaging consequences of this concentration on economic progress. The author agrees with Clarence Randall that we worship production. Monday through Friday we are so absorbed with it there is no room for another religion. We do reserve Sunday to recall the dear departed faith we honor but no longer rely on to help us in our really important activities. At the same time we have become vaguely aware of the malady that afflicts our society. The discontent with plenty and the restless searching for dependable values are symptoms of our distress.

"Skyhooks" is chiefly concerned with the effect of our religion of production upon industrial leadership. Mr. Ohmann notes that it obstructs natural man-to-man feeling in the handling of human relations. Social science is explored for techniques to process the human elements conformably with the logic of production. These efforts are futile, he thinks, although he concedes the social type of individual has been noticeably altered. Following David Riesman, he agrees that we have become an insecure, other-directed people. Management training has become more difficult since management itself is so strongly affected by other-directedness. The intensity of effort that goes into pleasing the superior leaves the individual drained of energy for personal convictions.

Thus "Skyhooks" has renewed some anxieties Dean Wallace B. Donham mentioned in *Education for Responsible Living* (1944). Loss of purpose in our national life in the period between the world wars had bothered him:

"Twenty years ago, in the period of great prosperity around 1923-27, I felt that this nation was one of the least stable nations on the face of the globe. I still feel that way. . . . In times of peace our capacity to work together, to cooperate, and our long term ideals for the nation were nearly lost. . . . We must refuse to accept dollar tests as final. There are more fundamental things to be thinking about."

If we are to halt the mischief Mr. Ohmann and others see, before we exhaust our resources of character and stamina, we must take pains to give management a broader outlook. Management must sense the world of the spirit and seek to serve it in order to produce balance and purpose in its own and the community outlook. In this connection we shall have to be careful about people with quick, comfortable, spiritual remedies. Cults of reassurance seem to be trying to adapt man to the defects of too much unassimilated economic progress. The fellows who want to save us with dated economics (whom Mr. Ohmann regards dubiously) are not the only ones to watch.

We are in need of a completely new revelation which will restore perspective. Economic progress must be maintained, but in a context which will permit managers and workers to develop wholeness of personality. After all, a social order which has to be sustained by the amount of satisfaction its economic system can produce is inherently unstable. Life is not given as ready-made. We need work which can help us develop our character and self-respect as well as our income.

Some of the things Mr. Ohmann recommends for change may take some time. We shall probably have to live with the trend toward bigness for quite a while—national defense requires it. But there may be some hope that jobs can be redesigned to provide the scope and challenge to help men develop character. Peter Drucker's series of articles in *Harper's* suggests that automation may presently make such a demand for high-grade talent that we may have to keep people past sixty-five in the work world. Whatever promise this holds, let us hope that we may be spared the anomaly of having to work at our pleasures, an alternative Riesman has observed in our other-directed society.

A better alternative might be the discovery of a mystic like Mr. Ohmann. The distinction and leadership his company has so long exhibited probably lies in its appreciation of a man who can speak with authority in the important field of the spirit. Adolf A. Berle, Jr., in *The 20th Century Capitalist Revolution,* says:

"There is solid ground for the expectation that 20 years from now the men of the greatest renown in the United States will be the spiritual, philosophical and intellectual leaders for the sufficient reason that they will be more needed than any other type. Society still tends to produce and to honor the kinds of men it needs most."

6.

The Roots of Business Responsibility

BY BERNARD W. DEMPSEY*

Two competent observers of American business, Donald K. David, former dean of the Harvard Graduate School of Business Administration, and John Maurice Clark, professor of economics, Columbia University, have addressed themselves to the problem of the constitution of our economy with characteristic vigor and originality and with impressive results.[1] Clark's analysis is couched in terms of "an alternative to serfdom," though his book is by no means a mere rebuttal of Hayek.[2] David thinks rather in terms of those responsibilities of businessmen which without reflection they have already practically assumed or which on reflection lie immediately to hand and for which they have the capacity and the inclination.

The problem fully merits the attention it is receiving at such hands as these. There exists a genuine conflict of economic systems, and if we do not make our own system work, the consequence is serfdom. This is not a time to permit minor prejudices, slogans, and clichés to substitute for sturdy, courageous thinking. Fortu-

---

* The Reverend Dempsey, S. J., is professor and director of the department of economics at Marquette University.

[1] Donald K. David, "Business Responsibilities in an Uncertain World," Supplement to *Harvard Business Review* (May 1949); John Maurice Clark, *Alternative to Serfdom* (New York, Alfred A. Knopf, Inc., 1948).

[2] Frederich Hayek, *Road to Serfdom* (Chicago, University of Chicago Press, 1944).

nately businessmen are ready for clear, sound, and genuinely radical thinking; though they are characteristically inarticulate, there is a "deep concern, almost a ferment, in the minds of many regarding the moral and ethical foundations of our industrial civilization."[3]

Both men attack directly "the great problems of freedom and responsibility, community and market mechanism, political and economic agency."[4] The results are impressive not only because of the standing of the writers but more so because of the intrinsic cogency of the reasoning itself and of the fundamental agreement that exists between the work of two independent students.

Although their ideas may seem to be at variance with some notions widely accepted today, they are thoroughly consistent with most fundamental and characteristic American attitudes. Moreover, the conclusions of both men strikingly agree with advanced business thinking which has wholly different intellectual roots; the empirical and the analytical concur in remarkable detail. The purpose of this article is to demonstrate this agreement and, by extending both types of thinking, to arrive at the principles in which the developing idea of business responsibility is rooted.

David's conclusions involve one general condition and two propositions. The general condition is the simple reality that the facts have far outrun the notion of "the economic man." The businessman is aware of this and is self-conscious and ill at ease when called on to discuss in public topics that lie beyond his own immediate experience. The practical man who really has something of his own to contribute is thus placed in the wholly indefensible position of expounding a theory he does not practice and of relating his experience to principles he does not really believe.

David's two propositions are (1) that the businessman has the ability to contribute notably to the general social welfare, and (2) that the businessman has the obligation to contribute to the general social welfare.

Clark's conclusions concern rather the social organization and the atmosphere within which the businessman and other eco-

---

[3] Donald K. David, *op. cit.*, p. 8.
[4] John Maurice Clark, *op. cit.*, p. vii.

nomic agents make their contributions. American social environment in the recent past has not made it easy for the businessman to recognize or to fulfill his social obligations. In general, therefore, Clark's position coincides with David's first general condition that the facts have outrun "economic man." But both men emphasize the existence of economic communities as entities which are distinct from the state, real and functioning and very important.

RESPONSIBILITY AND JUSTICE

Both men speak in terms of businessmen's responsibility. Responsibility can be of many kinds and degrees. But, properly speaking, I am responsible for something only if there exists a claim on somebody's part requiring me to perform or deliver. When the responsibility is such as to require me to deliver to another person or persons that which is in some sense "his" or "theirs," then the responsibility is also a formal obligation in justice. The kind of justice in which this obligation is owed depends on the sense in which the thing to be delivered may be said to be "his" to whom I owe it.

Some of the responsibilities to which David refers are obligations in various kinds of justice. He is in effect saying that businessmen are becoming vaguely aware of justice in a new form, that they are beginning to recognize and approve it.

Exchange Justice

In its simplest form of personal exchange, *quid pro quo,* the businessman not only accepts and approves justice but regards it as an indispensable condition for doing business. The businessman pays his just debts and expects others to pay their debts to him. He lives up to his contracts, written and oral. Even the economic man practiced exchange justice, and historically the business community has an incredibly high average in the practice of this virtue. Daily in the United States transactions involving enormous values are completed simply and expeditiously on the briefest kind of memos because businessmen take for granted the practice of exchange justice.

No matter what a businessman's actual standards may be, nobody dares speak out in favor of injustice. However hard a bargain a businessman may drive, he will go through whatever logical contortions are necessary to prove that the deal was not unjust. He does this because everybody recognizes that it is indispensable that men deal justly with one another in a modern industrial civilization. Thus far we are on incontestable ground. The whole practical question is about the scope and range of relationships that are to be governed by justice. Besides the simple exchange justice admitted and practiced scrupulously by all businessmen there are two other relationships discernible, both admitted and accepted by businessmen but lacking the clarity and sharp focus that exchange justice has in their minds. The pressure of our actual problems within and of an aggressively competitive system without is forcing us to be clearer about these other relationships.

Distributive Justice

Beyond the person-to-person relationship of exchange justice, there is the relationship of any organized community, particularly the civil state, to its individual members. This cannot be governed solely by exchange justice; the concept of justice must, and does, expand to what may be called distributive justice which the executive of the government of every society or community is bound to practice. Exchange justice has fairly accurate measurements of the obligations on each side. Distributive justice cannot operate at the dollar-for-dollar equality that is possible in exchange justice, but it does demand a proportionate equality. An example is found in the progressive income tax. Every businessman in practice admits and defends the importance of distributive justice; within his own company he tries to practice it, for instance, in planning vacation schedules or in designing a bonus or retirement program. He demands it in the administration of public affairs. He does not, however, grasp it so clearly as he does exchange justice, nor does he practice it so rigorously as he does the other virtue which he more fully understands. A violation of distributive justice is more likely to be described as something which is unfair rather than unjust.

General Justice

Besides the person-to-person relationship of exchange justice and the state-to-person relationship of distributive justice, there is an obvious third one, the relation of the person to the community, again referring primarily to the civil community or state but having its counterpart in every society. This has been called general justice because it can cover a wide variety of human actions. The first half of general justice—legal justice—is also commonly admitted by businessmen; except in the rare case of a very unwise, ill-considered, or hopelessly administered law, businessmen take it for granted that they obey the law. Legal justice is the form of general justice which binds us all to contribute to the community by observing the ordinances which are laid upon us by legitimate authority.

The things which are requisite for the establishment, maintenance, and improvement of a good community are not necessarily exhausted by the passage of laws. This is clearer, for example, in a new community on the frontier, which is as yet unorganized. Its members have the same need of the community and the same obligation to contribute to it that they will have when the organized community imposes specific ordinances on them. The same is true of a completely disorganized community as in time of war, civil disturbance, or public disaster. The absence of formal organization does not in any way absolve one from contributing to the community whatever is necessary for its proper function. And this same obligation remains binding on the individual citizen when the community is badly organized, when its laws, for example, fail to make it easy for the economic factors of production—labor, management, ownership—to cooperate in the production of the material goods and services which are the first condition of well-being. This fundamental obligation which is antecedent to legal justice binds every member of the community simply because he is a member of a community. We will call it contributive justice.

Contributive Justice

The concept of contributive justice was developed by the Jesuit economist, Henry Pesch. It is simply an elaboration to suit modern conditions of ideas as old as Aristotle and previously well developed by writers like the jurists of the Roman Law, Aquinas, Molina, Lessius, and de Lugo. Pesch used both the term "contributive justice" and the term "social justice." "Contributive" is preferable as being more descriptive and because the term "social justice" has been loosely applied to many things which have no relation to what we are discussing here.

The development of Pesch's analysis by the contemporary economists, Gundlach and Nell-Breuning, greatly influenced the social encyclicals of Pope Pius XI. The summary statements contained in these letters give us such compact epitomes that they are preferable to the originals for our present purpose. Nell-Breuning's last work in this field before the war was confiscated by the Nazi government and publicly burned.

In key statements of David's speech the verb "contribute" and the noun "contribution" occur eight times. For example: "These abilities . . . are the basis of the contribution which responsible business leadership can and must make to our society," and, "It must come from a genuine recognition by the leader that each member of his organization has something to contribute and needs to be given the opportunity to do so."[5] These two quotations are direct verbal statements implying a recognition and acceptance of contributive justice. Other expressions tantamount to these—e.g., "constructive participation"—occur in every paragraph after the introduction.

Two further elements, also mentioned by David, need to be added to this basic concept of contribution. The first is the paramount place accorded in American thought to "respect for the dignity of the individual . . . and the ultimate worth of the free human being."[6] The second is the dynamic factor in economic life to which contributive justice is peculiarly adapted: "A dynamic society is by definition a changing one, and it is only to be expected that new patterns of relationship among the various sectors of our society will develop."[7]

With these elements we have all the factors contained in the classic statement of contributive or social justice by Pope Pius XI in 1937:

In reality, besides commutative justice, there is also social [i.e., contributive] justice with its own set obligations, from which neither

[5] Donald K. David, *op. cit.*, pp. 3, 4.
[6] *Ibid.*, p. 2.
[7] *Ibid.*

employers nor workingmen can escape. Now it is of the very essence of social justice to demand from each individual all that is necessary for the common good. But just as in the living organism it is impossible to provide for the good of the whole unless each single part and each individual member is given what it needs for the exercise of its proper functions, so it is impossible to care for the social organism and the good of society as a unit unless each single part and each individual member —that is to say, each individual man in the dignity of his human personality—is supplied with all that is necessary for the exercise of his social functions. If social justice be satisfied, the result will be an intense activity in economic life as a whole, pursued in tranquillity and order. This activity will be proof of the health of the social body, just as the health of the human body is recognized in the undisturbed regularity and perfect efficiency of the whole organism.

This passage is a carefully worded statement, by a writer conscious of the responsibility that goes with his statements, of the essential characteristics of contributive justice as formulated by Pesch and his collaborators. All the basic elements of David's thought are here presented although in a somewhat different order:

1. The obligation and capacity to contribute.

2. The well-being of the individual human person as the goal of the business process.

3. Contributive justice as the dynamic virtue producing progress, adjustment, efficiency.

In Practice

Basically there are two sets of reasons why men are bound to practice contributive justice, which I shall here briefly indicate rather than attempt to establish by formal argument.

The first reason is that every man has need of community organization. It is indispensable to the maintenance, development, and perfection of his personality. The members are bound to contribute to the common good of every community to which they belong; yet the community has nothing to give its members but their own previous contributions. However, just as the exchange of surpluses due to specialization between two economic agents can result in a greater total utility for both, so the diversity of human capacities makes it possible for the sum total of human receipts from the community far to exceed the contributions. But be that as it may, since I have unconditional need of sound, dynamic communities —domestic, municipal, economic, religious, social, civil—I have also an unconditional obligation to contribute to the common good of each; from my contribution others can receive what they must have, just as I can receive what I must have only from their contributions.

Apart from the inefficiencies, ineptitudes, and cost involved, some of the uneasiness and apprehension over governmental operation of business arises from the vague realization of the fact that when the government takes over a function, men no longer make a direct contribution but in effect pay the government to do it for them. It is like buying a substitute for military service. The person who has need of the community and has the obligation to contribute to the community needs has put his obligation in a form that makes it remote from him personally. He will no longer have the knowledge, experience, or appreciation of the function in which he no longer actively participates. The contribution which he should make as an obligation in contributive justice will not be adequately substituted for by state action even though distributive justice is observed. As the Pope said in 1931:

It is indeed true, as history clearly proves, that owing to the change in social conditions, much that was formerly done by small bodies can nowadays be accomplished only by large corporations. None the less, just as it is wrong to withdraw from the individual and commit to the community at large what private enterprise and industry can accomplish, so too it is an injustice, a grave evil, and a disturbance of right order for a larger and higher organization to arrogate to itself functions which can be performed efficiently by smaller and lower bodies. This is a fundamental principle of social philosophy, unshaken and unchangeable, and it retains its full truth today. Of its very nature, the true aim of all social activity should be to help individual members of the social body, but never to destroy or absorb them.

The state should leave to these smaller groups the settlement of business of minor importance. It will thus carry out with greater freedom, power, and success the tasks that belong to it, because it alone can effectively accomplish these, directing, watching, stimulating, and restraining, as circumstances suggest or necessity demands.

This proposition is known as the "principle of subsidiarity." The meaning is that each higher society is subsidiary to the lesser societies within it; that is, the higher society must help the lesser ones to settle their own affairs, not settle those affairs for them. But this can only be done if the members of the lesser societies practice contributive justice. The enormous extension of state action into fields outside its competence is chiefly due to the absence of contributive justice among the members of the lesser societies within the state.

When the civil government takes over a function that men through the exercise of contributive justice could have done for themselves, there has been a failure of human growth. Men who turn their problems over to the state or allow the state to assume control of functions that could have been done on a contributive basis are less perfect men who have not used the capacity for organization, administration, and contribution that David has described as characteristic of today's businessman.

The simplest exercise of contributive justice is efficient production. In an ideally organized community this contribution is made easily, promptly, and with ample economic rewards.

The second basic reason for the existence of obligations in contributive justice is that the business enterprise controls resources which, like all natural resources, are designed for the sustenance of all men. The ultimate moral ground for the institution of private property is that it is, through exchange, the most efficient method of reducing resources to common use. Moreover, the large business enterprise pre-empts the services of men, services which are their only practical means of attaining access to resources which are designed for their sustenance as well as that of all other men. The same services are the only practical means these same men have of contributing to the community of which they also are a part. The more complex and elaborate the aggregates of capital become, the less immediate is the contact of the individual worker with the natural resources which are necessary to his life and growth. Though some of these modern aggregates of capital goods are incredibly efficient and therefore desirable, their presence and their complexity make more imperative the practice of contributive justice.

Since the resources used are ultimately designed to serve the common good, since the men employed on these resources have no other access to means of economic support, and since they have no other practical means of contributing to the economic society which is indispensable to them, it follows that there are, all around, obligations in contributive justice demanding the efficient conduct of economic society. As David says:

I feel strongly that operating a successful business is the first responsibility of a business leader. The simple fact is that in our society the businessman is primarily responsible for organizing the production and distribution of the nation's goods and services. He can meet that responsibility only through the competent management of business enterprise and through the creation and development of healthy business concerns. To me it is unrealistic to presume that the business leader can discharge any other responsibility if he fails in this, his foremost job.[8]

In short, as Pesch established, just as exchange justice is necessary for the conduct of individual transactions, and just as distributive and legal justice are necessary for the administration of the civil organization, so there is a form of justice—contributive—which is necessary for the organization and efficient conduct of economic activity.

BUSINESS AS A SOCIETY

This brings us to David's second point—that the businessman must make his enterprise a good society. A society is a permanent union of persons to achieve a common purpose. A business enterprise is such a union. In any society, for the expeditious management of its affairs authority is necessary; even when there is no question of right or wrong, authority is required to make decisions, to get things done, to choose among the various possible ends and among the numerous ways in which a given end may be reached. So authority is necessary in the business society known as the firm, just as in any other society.

Union of Equals

But in America, business managers and workers alike have accepted a groundless and alien concept of class conflict. This

[8] Donald K. David, *op. cit.*, p. 4.

theory—whatever may be said of Europe—finds no support in actual American business history. The facts must be squeezed and bent and twisted to give it even a semblance of plausibility. Though there have been, on occasions, sharp conflicts between employers and employees *as a matter of fact,* this is no evidence of an inevitable, irrepressible conflict *as a matter of principle.*

Marriage has been the occasion of conflict though it is normally a society with grave obligations in contributive justice. But these actual clashes cause no one to propound a theory of matrimony and the family based on essential conflict. The union of economic factors in efficient cooperation has a strong analogy to the family. The firm, like the family, is a union of equal persons with different but essential contributions.

Nevertheless, many Americans talk as though class conflict had to be taken for granted. Acceptance on the part of employers of this impractical Marxian abstraction has driven the men outside the company for their human satisfactions, for the acceptance, recognition, solidarity, and approbation in association with one's fellows which is essential even to the maintenance of mental health: "Man needs to belong to a community unit smaller and more personal than the overpowering state; but the units that meet this need—including trade unions—are not parts of an integrated community but monopolistic groups at war with others."[9] One of the major functions of American unions is to furnish a citadel and a platform from which it is safe to talk back to the boss.

David's presentation of the producing unit as a society, however, puts the matter in a different light. The distinction between the "company" and the "men" disappears. Both are absorbed in a functioning unit within which managers and workers alike can easily contribute to the common good of the producing society of which both are members. Authority must exist for the efficient conduct of business, but an authority exercised for the common good of all members of the society, whatever the nature of their contribution, cannot be reasonably resented and will not be. As he says:

Part of the businessman's competence lies in his ability to get people to work together for a common goal. It is here, as I see it, that the second

[9] John Maurice Clark, *op. cit.,* p. ix.

responsibility of business leadership arises—the responsibility for making his organization a "good society." Businessmen have known for a long time—almost instinctively—that the people under them had to "work together." Many, however, knew little and cared less how those people felt as long as the business "got results," i.e., produced economic satisfactions.

In every business I see opportunity unlimited for improving the "human" satisfactions which—I sincerely believe—people have a right to expect from the place where they spend as much as a quarter of their lives, their place of employment. If we could ever develop the technique, the background, the knowledge—just for instance—so that the right man could be in the right job, just think of the frustrations, the unhappiness, the economic and social waste which could be avoided.[10]

The company—a stable association of investors, managers, office and production employees—is the society within which most economic agents normally find the means of making their economic contribution to the community. By the same token the firm is the agency by which private property and personal abilities are made to serve their twofold masters—their owners and the community of which the owners are members. But the firm is a society. It must be governed by its managers for the common good of the whole society. To regard as metaphysical enemies two groups that are in daily active cooperation in the efficient production of goods is as unreal as it is costly.

Interdependence

Yet the firm as the ultimate economic society is obviously not without its own obligations and its rights in contributive justice. Businesses are interdependent—horizontally, vertically, and in the many intertwining ways that Alfred Marshall lumped under "external economies." The company, as a society to which its members contribute and which contributes to its members, has rights to efficient service from its suppliers and obligations of efficient service to its customers. Apart from those actively contributing within the firm, the customers are the firm's chief practical contact with the community.

The firm as a whole must therefore be governed not merely for

[10] Donald K. David, *op. cit.*, p. 4.

the common good of all its members but also for the common good
of the other communities of which it is in turn a member and to
which it must contribute. These communities are, first of all, the
industry to which the firm belongs and, second, the municipal
community within which it operates. And each industry is in turn
similarly obligated to the other industries. As Clark says:

> The price of freedom is its responsible exercise. . . . Whenever man
> acts as an individual, he is responsible to his group or his community;
> and when he acts on behalf of his group, he is responsible to the members
> of the groups he represents; and on behalf of the group he is responsible
> to his community—to the whole society or to some larger constituent
> group of which the first group is a member.[11]

REGULATORS OF THE ECONOMY

But what is the relation of contributive justice to the theory that
competition is the primary and principal regulator of the economy? No one can deny the value of competition as a stern dis-
ciplinarian of the economically inefficient or as the distributor of
substantial rewards to the intelligent, the industrious, and the
lucky. But actually the typical American businessman does not
operate under textbook competition, nor does he believe in it.
Whatever may have been its validity under small-scale, owner-
operated production, it no longer functions according to the
diagrams.

Competition Only Secondary

Competition is an important and useful secondary regulator
of the economy. But it must operate within an economic community already organized. Contributive justice is the first principle
of economic organization; it imposes a positive obligation on every
economic agent not only to contribute positively to every community of which he is a member but to contribute positively to
the formation of necessary communities which do not exist. Those
economists who bewail the passing of the frontier do not realize
that American economic life is still on the frontier of community
organization; one of our urgent obligations is to form realistic
economic communities. The entrepreneur uses resources on which

[11] John Maurice Clark, *op. cit.*, p. 4.

the whole community has an ineradicable claim; he pre-empts personal services which represent the only form in which workers can make economic contributions to their communities and establish claims proportionate to their contributions. So he must accept the responsibilities of contributive justice and compete, however strenuously, within an organized market. According to David:

At the same time the leader of one of these units is a participant in a larger organization. His performance in that larger group depends substantially on the degree of participation he has been able to encourage from those who make up the social unit of which he is the head. Thus, it is through the exercise of his skills—his administrative talent and his competence in judging risks and taking wise actions—within the framework of the social unit with which he is directly concerned that the business executive is enabled to make a contribution to the larger unit of which he is a part.

Now I have set forth at some length this concept because I think it is useful when we come to examine the third quality which I believe necessary to a business leader, namely, his constructive participation in the broader affairs of his community and nation.[12]

Business thinking today is in a "ferment" because businessmen feel that theoretical individualism offers them no place to put their feet and that the only apparent alternative to theoretical individualism is state control, which is clearly the road to serfdom.

Because men have regarded competition as a primary and sufficient regulator of the economy and have not demanded contributive justice of economic agents, the state has rushed into the vacuum thus created. However useful competition may be in disciplining established fair markets, it has demonstrated little capacity to establish such markets and less capacity to create an economic community of self-governing societies. Clark says:

Economically we are not a community. The market has had such marvelous organizing powers that it has deluded many of us, for some hundred and seventy years, into thinking that it could do all that was needed to organize an economic community on a basis of consent as embodied in the act of free exchange. But it has been growingly evident for many years that this was expecting from it something beyond its

12 Donald K. David, *op. cit.,* p. 5.

powers, great as these were. We have gradually discovered—though many have not admitted it—that markets can organize material interests only, and not all of these, and that this is not enough to constitute a society. . . . Things the market pseudo-society has wrecked are hopefully turned over to the state, a too vast and impersonal mechanism whose constitution does not correspond too well to the economic realities.

Between the individual and government, or markets, stand great organized groups; farm federations, business corporations, and labor unions. And these are the crux of the present dilemma. In a simple economy without such groups, irresponsible self-interest is—almost—a possible organizing principle in the strictly material realm. It would merely mean the exploitation of the weak by the strong, the incapable by the capable. But organize society into groups and irresponsible self-interest can both corrupt the groups and shatter the society.[13]

The union, the trade association, and the farm federation represent the expression of a normal inclination to association and contribution that has been distorted by the acceptance of "class consciousness," which thwarts the normal inclination of reasonable men to function as members of a community and contribute to its well-being. This strained condition is, according to O. H. Taylor's summary of Clark's position, the product of the "illusion that the truly great organizing power of the free market system was so great as to be able to accomplish all needful organizing of society as distinguished from the state." Taylor goes on to say:

As those conflicts grow increasingly acute with the growing power and sophistication of every group, and increasingly disrupt and distort the operation of the market mechanism, we tend to enlarge the coercive powers and functions of the state and look to it to control the groups. . . . Liberty can be saved only by an adequate growth of responsibility in its exercise by all individuals and groups.[14]

Examples in History

There are not lacking in American business history examples of attempts to institutionalize contributive justice. The old New York Stock Exchange was a formal organization of a market on a voluntary basis with very high standards of both exchange and

---

[13] John Maurice Clark, *op. cit.*, pp. 4, 5.
[14] "Economics of a Free Society, Four Essays," *Quarterly Journal of Economics*, November 1948, p. 657.

contributive justice in recognition of a public responsibility. The movie industry and the baseball industry are peculiar, special cases of industries with unusual public responsibilities that have imposed on their members obligations of contributing to the common good of the industry and the community. Whatever their faults, it would be difficult to find two more peculiarly American businesses than movies and baseball.

Regardless of what he may say when discussing "the old fundamentals" at a Chamber of Commerce dinner, the American business executive has a strong personal inclination to contributive justice. He devotes valuable time to community projects—community funds and the like—because he has a vague feeling that it is the right thing to do. In other words, the operation of contributive justice can be so obvious that it is practiced even when not fully understood. During the war, there were dollar-a-year men who devoted their administrative talents to public service without compensation, and there were many older men who overworked on war production in their own plants to the point of serious exhaustion and in a few cases even to death. If you had asked them why they did this, they would have been unable to give you a clear and simple reason. The reason of course was the recognition that in time of crisis contributive justice "demands from each individual all that is necessary for the common good." And the demand is accepted and met in the same way that a man pays his debts.

At the depth of the depression an industrialist of great influence sternly rebuked a banker who had refused additional loans to a greatly embarrassed university. When the industrialist pointed out that such loans are made even when the prospects of repayment are bad because the university is part of the community, he was practicing contributive justice; the banker was not.

GUIDING PRINCIPLE

The American business leader is badly in need of a principle to guide his actions, to channel his natural inclination and capacity for contribution, and to give him a formula for achieving those things which he thinks need to be done but which he is properly afraid to hand over to the civil state. The mental effort of our best business analysts is combining with traditional analysis to give it to him.

Contributive justice is such a principle preparing the way for a progressive, realistic, "town meeting" brand of business economics. I say "town meeting" advisedly because justice like charity begins at home and, if it is to be effective, must operate on the plant level. The principle of subsidiarity holds it down in the first instance to practical operation on the plant level.

Readers of these paragraphs, though inclined to accept the principle of contributive justice, may also be inclined to question its practical value. Well, we are dealing here with a principle, a very real and true principle, but a broad one capable of the greatest adaptability in application. Principles are important even when we cannot foresee all of their applications. For example, when atomic energy was first released under laboratory conditions, a principle of immense importance had been verified. There were no doubt people who, hearing that a group of scientists had achieved nuclear fission, asked: "So what? What good is it? Can you run an automobile with it, or heat your house with it?" This same sort of person would want immediately to make a blueprint of an economic constitution just because we have established a social principle that is as important in its own order as the principle of nuclear fission in its order.

In this matter of nuclear fission, once the principle had been verified, there remained a tremendously difficult, important, and impressive engineering problem. This was the job of making an atomic bomb small enough to be carried in an airplane and accurate enough not only to release atomic energy but also to release it in the few seconds required for the bomb to fall from the plane to the earth. Such a job on the engineering level was quite as impressive as the scientific job on the analytical level. Other grave engineering problems remain. No one can say today what the ultimate practical applications of the release of atomic energy are. But that does not make the principle unimportant.

David and Clark have arrived empirically at a principle or set of principles of the first order of significance. Their findings dovetail with the results of serious investigations approaching the problems in wholly different ways and reorienting some of the best thinking in Western culture. Moreover, the principles uncovered offer a sane and intelligent outlet for the best instincts of the American businessman. These results may indeed in their own order be as radical as the release of atomic energy was in theoretical physics. Yet the job of social engineering that remains to be done to reduce these principles to daily practical application may be quite as formidable as were the engineering problems involved in applying the pure principles of nuclear physics. But clearly the times forbid that we should not make the attempt.

7.

Religious Foundations of Economic Progress

By Kenneth E. Boulding*

One of the most challenging—and most tantalizing—propositions of what may be called the "larger economics" is that the success of economic institutions depends to a large extent upon the nature of the whole culture in which they are embedded, and not on the nature of these institutions in themselves. This proposition is of particular importance in two current fields of economic inquiry: (a) the study of the complex forces which underlie economic development and (b) the study of the stability and survival power of the characteristic institutions of capitalism.

Indeed, it is only a slight exaggeration to say that the wealth of a nation is a by-product of certain elements in its culure, cumulated through the years. Over a broad range of human societies within the extremes of the Eskimo and the desert nomad, if one area is rich and another poor, it is not because of anything inherent in the natural resources or in the genetic make-up of the people, but because of the cumulative effect of certain familial, educational, and religious practices. Thus the forbidding soil and climate of New England provided a comfortable—if not opulent —homeland for the Puritan, while under the Turk, in his unspeakable days, the ancient cradles of civilization became barren and starveling deserts.

Of all the elements of culture which shape economic institutions,

* Mr. Boulding is professor of economics at the University of Michigan.

religious practices particularly play a key role—a doubly important one because many other elements of the pattern of life, such as sex, child rearing, work habits, agricultural and industrial practices, are themselves profoundly affected by the prevailing religious beliefs. That religion plays such an important role is not, however, sufficiently recognized by most people, and it is my purpose here to throw more light on it. More specifically, I shall attempt to survey certain aspects of our own society in the light of the contribution which religious ideas, practices, and institutions have made to its economic development and to its power of survival.

ECONOMIC DEVELOPMENT

To appraise the role of religion in economic development, we must understand the process by which economic change takes place. All change may not be for the better, but it is clear that there can be no betterment without some change.

Improvement Process

There are, then, three essential features of any process of economic development in a society—innovation, imitation, and displacement; and two further features which, though conceivably not indispensable, are almost certain to be present in any kind of economic improvement process of which we have knowledge—accumulation of capital and limitation of population. Let us look more closely at these five features:

(1) There must be an *innovator,* who first makes the change. He can be divided, as was done by Schumpeter, into an inventor and an entrepreneur. But the point here is that whether the function is specialized or not, or whether it is performed by a single individual or by a number, the function itself is necessary. If we are to have progress, somebody, somewhere, must do something in a way that has never been done before.

(2) If, however, there is no freedom to *imitate* a change—still more, if the innovator himself is suppressed by the conservative institutions of his society—there can be no testing out of the innovation to see whether it in fact constitutes a "betterment" or not. It would be rash to say that all innovations which are widely imitated are in fact "betterments," for even the mass may be wrong. But we can say that unless there is opportunity for imitation, an innovation *cannot* be tested, and nobody can

ever find out whether it is in fact a "good" innovation, that is, a "better" way of doing things.

(3) Imitation cannot take place, in turn, unless there is *displacement* of the old methods. It is the resistance to displacement (that is, to "competition") on the part of those whose interests are bound up with the old ways, and who are not flexible enough in their habits or opportunities to change, which is likely to be one of the main obstacles to change.

(4) Next, practically all economic innovation of which we have knowledge involves the *accumulation of capital,* in the broad sense of the increase in "valuable objects." The objects so accumulated are not only material; the acquisition of skills, traits, and abilities constitutes capital accumulation just as much as does the stockpiling of materials and material equipment.

If capital is to be accumulated, production must exceed consumption —production being gross additions to the total stock of capital, and consumption being subtractions from it. Such accumulation is far from automatic. In poor societies it is difficult because the minimum needs of consumption press daily on the meager and hard-won product; most of the activity of the society is concerned with mere maintenance, and little is left for accumulation. In rich societies the threat may be from more subtle sources—from unwillingness to accumulate (i.e., to invest) leading to unemployment and from levels of production below the society's capacity.

(5) Even if there is an increase in the total capital or income of a society, however, economic progress will not necessarily result. Economic well-being must rise on a per capita basis. Hence the accumulation of capital will not constitute "improvement" unless capital increases, in some sense, faster than population. And hence a permanent high-level economy is not possible unless there is *limitation of population*—that is, unless population is checked by methods other than starvation and poverty (according to the familiar "dismal theorem" of Malthus that if nothing checks the growth of population but misery and starvation, then the population will grow until it is miserable and starves).

Even if a society starts on the road of economic improvement, then, there are many elements in its culture which may prevent the improvement in techniques from resulting in an actual improvement in welfare. The newly won powers may be used merely for the support of larger populations at the old level of poverty, or they may also be squandered in the luxury of a foolish ruling class or in the waste of total war. The pyramids of Egypt and the endless wars of Rome are good examples of the waste of resources liberated by technical improvement.

THE PROTESTANT ETHIC

The past three centuries have witnessed a rate of economic development in the Western world which, measured by any standard we choose, almost certainly exceeds the achievement of any other period of equal length in human history. We are so much accustomed to this rapid progress, both in techniques and in general levels of income, that we are likely to take it for granted. Nevertheless, looking over the whole range of human history and prehistory, we can clearly see that these last three hundred years represent an episode in human development which has no parallel, except perhaps in that dim period when settled agriculture was invented and gave rise to the first civilizations.

The unique nature of the achievement makes it all the more important that we should not take it for granted, but should inquire very carefully into its sources in the culture of the Western world. The history of civilizations reveals that it is perfectly possible, indeed easy, to dry up the springs of progress in a society, and that virtually all past civilizations have eventually done so. Therefore, unless we are aware of the nature of those elements in our total pattern of life which are responsible for this rapid rate of development, we may run into grave danger of changing that pattern, without knowing it, in a way that destroys those peculiar elements in the culture from which development springs.

Important among the elements in our complex culture having favorable influence on the rate of economic development are certain religious ideas and practices which comprise the so-called "Protestant ethic."

The thesis of Max Weber and his school that the Protestant ethic has influenced the development of capitalism is now well accepted. Though one's estimate of the quantitative importance of this influence will depend to a great extent on the interpretation of history which one favors, the direction of the influence can hardly be in doubt.

What has not, I think, been pointed out with sufficient force is that the Protestant ethic has contributed to the *success* of capitalist institutions, particularly in regard to their fostering a high rate of economic progress. Economic sociologists like Weber, Sombart, and

Tawney, who have emphasized the close connection between religious and economic ideas, have been on the whole unfriendly to capitalist institutions and have consequently tended to lay stress on their failures rather than their successes. This is perhaps because the ethical systems of these writers were conceived in fairly static terms—in terms, for instance, of the problem of justice in the distribution of a given total income, rather than in terms of the encouragement of a growing total income.

It has now become clear, however, that the consequence of even a small rate of economic progress, persistently raising average incomes, is so enormous over even a few decades that from the point of view of long-run human welfare the capacity of a system to generate economic development has come to overshadow all other criteria in judging it "good" or "bad." (Curiously enough, this has also become true of Communism; in the interest of inducing a rapid rate of economic development the rulers of Russia have thrown overboard practically every other idea of their ethical system, and have developed degrees of inequality which even the most uncontrolled period of capitalist development could hardly rival.)

In other words, we see now that in practice the abolition of poverty can come only from development—not from redistribution, not from taking from the rich to give to the poor, but by making everybody richer. And it is on this score that the Protestant ethic, which was born with the Reformation, has been so influential.

Innovation in Religion

Innovation, imitation, and displacement in economic life have their counterparts in religious life. Thus the Reformation marked the beginning of a series of innovations in religion. Men like Martin Luther, John Calvin, Menno Simons, George Fox, John Wesley, General Booth, and even in our own day Frank Buchman, represent a disturbance of the previously established equilibrium, with a new form of religious enterprise and new arrangements of human time and spiritual energy. They are widely imitated, and the spread of the new technique forces profound adjustments even in those older institutions which do not go over completely to the new ideas.

It generally seems to be true that these innovations in religion have preceded and in some sense paved the way for innovations in economic life. Indeed, the most important innovation in any society is the *idea* of innovation itself, for this represents the Rubicon between the traditional stationary type of society, in which each generation repeats the pattern of its elders, and the "economic," dynamic society, in which innovation becomes an accepted and profitable role. A strong case can be made out for the claim that the principal historical agency bringing about this critical change is a reformation (or revolution) in religion, that this liberates the society from its previous equilibrium and exposes it to all the terrors and delights of dynamics. Once iconoclasm has succeeded in the most traditional and "sacred" area of life, once "free enterprise" has been successful in religion, the spirit of innovation seizes on all other areas of life.

What in our Western society we call *the* Reformation is of course only one among many. The period of rapid innovation which followed the rise of Mohammedanism is another and spectacular example. Within Christianity itself the monastic reformations—especially of the Benedictines and Cistercians—paved the way for the economic development of medieval Europe. Again —if only to remind us that Protestantism is not the whole story— the Counter Reformation within the Catholic Church also represents a period of "innovation," though of a less dramatic and less iconoclastic nature.

Individual Responsibility

The fact remains that the Protestant Reformation has certain specific features of its own which have increased its importance for economic development. I am not referring to the sanctification of economic activity through the extension of the concept of "vocation," as emphasized by earlier writers. The concept of vocation is not peculiar to Protestantism, nor is it so important as what I have in mind.

First of all, there is the "unmediated" character of Protestant religion, that is, the emphasis on the individual's own responsibility for his religious life and salvation without the intermediary of priest or prescribed ritualistic "works." It is this unmediated quality of Protestant religion which underlies the sociological significance of the doctrine of justification by faith. Protestantism, that is to say, represents private enterprise in religion, as opposed to the great organized collectivism of the Catholic Church.

It is not surprising that private enterprise in religion carried over into the economic field. The full effect of this is seen in the eighteenth century, where the immense economic innovations which constituted the beginnings of the technical revolution in banking, trade, and industry were to an astonishing extent the work of the British Nonconformists, and especially of the Quakers, who had developed the most unmediated of all Protestant varieties of religion.

Perfectionism

Another aspect of Protestantism which relates closely to economic development is its perfectionism. Like the earlier monastic reformations, Protestantism reflects a discontent with compromise with the "world" and a serious attempt to return to the pristine revelation of perfection implied in the Christian vision of perfect love. Unlike the monastic reformation, however, the Protestant Reformation—because one of the things against which it was protesting was the corruption of the monastery and nunnery prevalent in the time of Luther—rejected the monastic solution and became an attempt to lead the life of Christian perfection in the workaday world rather than in cloistered separation.

Such an attempt, however, is almost doomed to fail, and the difficulty of practicing the major virtue of charity will lead to an insensible substitution of the "minor virtues" as attainable ends of the religious group. So the perfectionist subsides into the Puritan, and groups of people arise practicing, with some success, the minor virtues of thrift, hard work, sobriety, punctuality, honesty, fulfillment of promises, devotion to family, and so on. The minor virtues, however, lead almost inevitably to accumulation and increased productivity, and eventually therefore to an escape from poverty.

The Lost Economic Gospel

This all adds up to what I call the "lost economic gospel" of Protestantism. Poverty is the result of "sin," sin being defined in terms of intemperance, loose living, prodigality, laziness, dishonesty, and so on (that is, in terms of violation of the "minor virtues").[1] On yielding to the power of Christ and the discipline of the congregation the individual is converted, gives up his evil ways, and becomes temperate, frugal, thrifty, hard working, honest, and so on; as a result of which he begins to accumulate skill and other capital and raises his standard of life. Thus he becomes respectable, and incidentally, but only incidentally, he may become rich by hitting on a successful innovation.

In the process of the individual's becoming richer, society also becomes richer. Indeed, the improvement of society is nothing more than the sum of the improvements of individuals. In a dynamic and improving society, therefore, the increase in riches of the individual is not thought of as a redistribution of wealth (one individual gaining at the expense of others) but rather as a creation of wealth (the gains of one individual representing net additions to the total and being taken from no man). Economic life is not a "zero sum" poker game in which a fixed volume of wealth is circulated around among the players, but a "positive sum" enterprise in which the accumulation of each person represents something which he brings to the "pot" rather than something which he takes out.

Another doctrine which Protestantism shares with other forms of Christianity has combined with the "lost gospel" to contribute to the success of capitalist institutions: the doctrine of stewardship, of charity in the narrower sense of the word. Those whose virtue, energy, or plain good fortune have brought them material success are expected to regard their riches as in some sense a trust, to be used for the benefit of the less fortunate. Over the long pull, this aspect of Christian culture has proved of great importance in modifying the inequalities of capitalism. As in the Middle Ages the establishment of monasteries was an important agency in the redistribution of wealth and income, so in the nineteenth and twentieth centuries the establishment of universities and foundations has provided a means whereby private accumulations have found their way into public uses.

The habit of mind engendered by the doctrine of stewardship has

---

[1] Kenneth E. Boulding, "Our Lost Economic Gospel," *The Christian Century*, August 16, 1950, pp. 970-972.

also been important in removing obstacles to legislative methods of correcting inequalities, such as progressive income and inheritance taxation. It is quite possible that this factor may have something to do with the different impact of capitalist institutions in the West and, say, in China, where the acquisitive opportunities have been less likely to be modified by the sense of responsibility for the welfare of those outside the circle of kinship.

It can hardly be doubted, then, that the "lost gospel"—the old gospel of individualism, of self-help—is in many respects a sound one. Indeed, the middle-class nature of Protestantism is a testimony to its long-run success. If Protestants are middle-class, it is largely because their Protestantism has made them so—has developed a culture in which hard work, thrift, family limitation, productivity, and frugality have been important values. There is hardly any better over-all recipe for economic development, whether for the individual or for a society.

Decline of Old Doctrines

Nevertheless, to a considerable degree the old doctrines are discredited in the churches today, especially, oddly enough, in the more prosperous ones. The old gospel of self-help flourishes among the little rising sects, the pentecostal people, and the store-front churches; it is actually the poor who seem to be least aware of the new "social gospel" and who cling to the old-time individual virtues. In the large Protestant denominations, as represented by the National Council of Churches, it is not perhaps unfair to say that there is more awareness of the weakness of the individualist gospel than of its strength, and that even where the older gospel is preached, it is often the result of the momentum of tradition rather than of any continuing spiritual insight.

There are significant reasons for the decline of the gospel of self-help and the rise of the "social gospel." Part of the cause lies in sheer misunderstanding, stemming from failure to appreciate the ethical significance of economic progress, and a resultant economic ethic based on static assumptions, in which an undue stress is laid on distributing a fixed sum of wealth fairly rather than on increasing the total to be distributed.

More fundamental is a certain inevitable tension between the ethic of the New Testament and the ethic of Samuel Smiles (the old Scottish biographer of industrialists and extoller of thrift and self-reliance). There is an antieconomic strain in the teaching of almost all the prophets and poets. The careful, calculating economizing way of life is neither prophetic nor poetic. It counts the cost; it asks for reward; it has no fine frenzies; it is humdrum, commonplace, even a little sordid. The stimulus to economic progress, therefore, is not in the ethic of the New Testament itself; rather it is in the "Puritan" substitute-ethic, the product of the impact of the ethic of love on the iron laws of the world.

The substitute-ethic, however, is itself somewhat unstable, because it is always subject to criticism by the pure ethic which generates it. Hybrids are vigorous but can generally only be reproduced from pure stock! Thus when the New Testament makes a fresh impact on a sensitive and vigorous mind—as it is likely to do at least once in a generation—the gospel of "be righteous and grow rich," for all its truth and practicality, looks cheap and pharisaical beside the poetic vision of "sell all thou hast and give to the poor"; and radical forms of Christianity tend to appear. There is something in Toynbee's suggestion that Communism is a Christian heresy!

Weaknesses of Capitalism

Perhaps a still more fundamental reason for the failure of capitalism to sustain the ethic which supports its most characteristic institutions is to be found in certain technical failures of these institutions themselves.

The ethic of capitalism is based firmly on the proposition that wealth is produced by saving and that saving is accomplished by producing much and consuming little. That is why the principal recipe for riches includes hard work and thrift and the other Protestant virtues. Under some circumstances, however, wealth is not produced by saving. Hard work works the worker out of a job, parsimony produces unemployment, and the fluctuations of the price system redistribute wealth without regard to any of the soberer virtues. The thrifty and hard-working find their net worth disappearing in deflation and their hard-earned interest and pensions evaporating in inflation, while the speculator and the manipulator reap what others have sown.

In conditions of general price and output instability the poker-game aspects of capitalism come to the fore. Instead of wealth being accumulated by carefully contributing to the physical stock more than one takes from it, it is accumulated by taking advantage of the shifting structure of relative values, by buying cheap and selling dear. Every economist will recognize, of course, that there is a legitimate function of speculation, and that some flexibility of the price structure is necessary to reflect changing structures of productivity and tastes. In fact, however, the characteristic institutions of capitalism—especially the organized commodity and security markets and the real estate market—have lent themselves to fluctuations far beyond what the flexibility of the system requires, and have therefore been the instrument of redistributions of wealth which have created a gap between economic virtue (in the sense of contribution to the progress of real wealth) and reward.

The phenomenon of depression has been particularly destructive to the capitalist ethic, because the misery which it has entailed has seemed to be so meaningless: why work and save when the end result is the foreclosure of a mortgage and selling apples in the street! The whole technical weakness of an ungoverned market economy can be summed up in two concepts: (a) speculative instability in price levels due to the dynamics of self-justified expectations, and (b) the limited or imperfect market resulting either from monopolistic imperfections in the market structure or from general deflation. Speculative instability leads to essentially meaningless redistributions of wealth. The limited market leads to an undue shift of emphasis away from production, to wasteful advertising and selling costs, to restrictions of output, to feather-bedding, and to other familiar devices by which individuals or segments of the economy seek to protect themselves from the impact of general deflations or seek to enhance their own particular power position at the expense of others.

The all-important question is whether these defects are to be regarded as diseases of the free economy, potentially curable within the general framework of market institutions, or whether they are to be regarded as essential genetic characteristics of it, quite incurable without a radical overthrow of the whole market economy itself.

CHANCES OF SURVIVAL

It is in this connection that the contribution of Keynes to the survival of capitalism is so important, for it is the essence of the Keynesian view that the defects of capitalism are curable diseases rather than incurable deformities. While the actual cures may be a matter still in considerable dispute, it is the great virtue of the Keynesian analysis that it gives us a clearer picture than we have ever had before of the nature of the disease, and it has consequently engendered the hope that institutions can be devised within the general framework of a free market economy which will prevent deflation and unemployment, on the one hand, and inflation, on the other.

If such a "governor" can insure the over-all stability of the economy (it is not the purpose of this discussion to say how this should be done), most of the ethical objections to a market economy fall to the ground. Given a reasonable degree of stability of the over-all price and output system, the old-fashioned virtues of hard work, thrift, honesty, and so on come into their own.

Underdeveloped Areas

Perhaps the crucial test of the capitalist system will turn on its ability to solve what is by far the greatest single economic problem facing the world today: the development of the so-called under-developed areas—inhabited by about three-quarters of the world's population—to the point where at least the grim consequences of extreme poverty (malnutrition, early death, constant ill health, superstition, squalor, and misery) are mitigated.

There are, roughly speaking, two kinds of society in the world today. The "high-level" societies have low birth and death rates, an expectation of life at birth rising up toward 60 or 70 years, disease well under control, malnutrition rare, literacy universal, education widespread, a high status and much freedom for women, complex economic and political institutions, and so on. The "low-level" societies, on the other hand, have high birth and death rates, an expectation of life around 30 years, disease and malnutrition rampant, literacy and education confined to a small upper class, a low status for women among the mass of the people, burdensome and exploitative financial institutions, often a colonial status, and so on.

The crux of the problem is how to raise the three-quarters of the world that live on a low level to the high level of the other quarter, for it is precisely this wide disparity that makes our world so unstable. American-Russian relations, for instance, would not constitute the apparently insoluble problem which they now pose if the relationship were simply one of America and Russia; in that event they could perfectly well leave each other alone! The relationship is complicated almost unbearably by the fact that each power is competing for the support of the vast fringe of underdeveloped countries which divide them on the globe, from Poland to China. Many countries are dissatisfied with their present state and are hovering between the two cultures, wondering which offers them the best chance of shifting from their present low-level to a high-level economy.

In this whole difficult situation it is of vital importance to appreciate the relation of economic institutions and economic development to the *whole* culture pattern, and to realize that the success of any set of economic institutions depends on the total culture setting in which they are placed. The success, even of modern technology, therefore, may depend quite as much on the missionary as on the engineer. One of the tasks of human inquiry is to discover exactly what the elements are in any culture which perpetuate poverty—whether in family life, in religious life, in education, in politics, or in economic and financial institutions— and then to effect the *minimum* change in the culture which is necessary to eradicate these germs of poverty.

We do not want, of course, the kind of cultural imperialism that insists on giving the Fiji Islanders Coca-Cola and Christmas trees whether these things are meaningful extensions of their present culture or not. Cultural change and cultural impact, however, there must be. Such impact is immensely dangerous and may result in disaster to both cultures; yet with the collapse of isolation such impact is inevitable. If it is to be ultimately fruitful, it must be understood much better than we understand it now; the marriage of economics and cultural anthropology must be accomplished, even at the point of a shotgun!

Danger of Social Sciences

It must not be thought, however, that all that is needed for world salvation is a stiff dose of social science, no matter how well documented empirically and no matter how well integrated analytically. The rise of social science presents man with problems of an ethical and spiritual nature of which he is still for the most part not aware. The spectacular "success" of the physical sciences in expanding the power of man, both for good and for evil, is dramatically symbolized in the atom bomb. The worst that a physicist can do for anybody, however, is to cause pain and death. The social scientist, when he knows a little more, may be able to destroy the soul, that inner core of freedom and integrity which constitutes at once the humanity and the divinity of man.

The nightmare of the "manipulative society"—the brave new world of Aldous Huxley or George Orwell—is not too far from reality. We see it foreshadowed in the crudely manipulative society of Soviet Russia, and it is this aspect of Communism which rightly fills us with disgust and fear. In its very conflict with Communism, however, the West may find itself sliding imperceptibly into a manipulative society more horrible, because more efficient, than the Soviet counterpart.

A world of unseen dictatorship is conceivable, still using the forms of democratic government, in which education has been replaced by training, in which government creates artificially the public opinion which keeps it in power, in which "loyalty" investigations corrupt the whole system of communications, in which only "safe" ideas are expressed, in which love of country is corroded by conscription and integrity is swallowed up in expediency, and in which the springs of technical, as well as of moral, progress are eventually dried up. The cleverer we are and the more we know, the more thoroughly we may damn ourselves.

RELIGION AS GUIDE

When the final history of the human race comes to be written, therefore, the part played by religion and religious experience may be even more significant than I have suggested earlier. I have argued that religion is an important autonomous force in the development of the technical revolution. It may turn out to be even more important in the control of this revolution.

We do not yet realize, I believe, what a portentous watershed in human history we are now treading. Civilization is a product of the increase in human control over environment which resulted from the invention of settled agriculture. All past civilizations, however, have proved to be unstable; the "iron laws" of social dynamics have eventually caught up with them and destroyed them. It is by no means improbable that our own civilization will suffer the same fate.

Yet there is reason for hope. As our knowledge not only of nature but of man and society expands, we may get to the point where man comes not to be ruled by history but to rule it. He may be able to take the iron laws and fashion them into an instrument for his own purposes, to mold the unconscious dynamic which drives him to destroy his civilizations into a conscious dynamic which will empower him to perpetuate them indefinitely.

The possibility of permanent and universal civilization therefore rises before us, though the prospect is not necessarily one to be approached without fear. It might be the kingdom of heaven on earth, but it might also be an indestructible and universal tyranny, securely based on the power of both physical and social science. A world of refugees is bad enough, but a world in which there is no place of refuge would be worse.

An increase in human power, therefore, makes all the more urgent the question of the discipline of the human will. Economic development means an increase in our ability to get what we want. Religion, however, raises the question of whether we want the right things. As long as we are impotent, it does not perhaps matter so much in regard to externals whether we want the right things or the wrong things. We cannot get what we want in any case. But if we can get what we want, the question of whether we want the right things becomes acutely important.

There are those who think that as economic development comes to fruition in a humanistic heaven on earth where war, poverty, and disease are abolished, religion will wither away. In that mil-

lennium faith will be swallowed up in knowledge, hope in fulfillment, and love in psychoanalysis and group dynamics! Such a belief seems to be naïve. As power and knowledge increase, the question of the *truth* of religion—of what is the "will of God," and how
it is discovered and incorporated into the human will—becomes all-
important. The feather of religious experience may then tip the
great scales toward either heaven or hell on earth.

8.

The Cultural Crisis of Our Age

By Reinhold Niebuhr*

In every age practical men of affairs, no matter how pressing their immediate duties and how interesting their practical activities, have looked up from their daily tasks to ask questions both about the fate of the total human enterprise, or at least of their culture and civilization, and about the meaning of human existence itself, including their own existence. These questions are usually defined as "spiritual" questions, though they might better be described as "ultimate" questions in contrast to the immediate problems which press upon us in our daily tasks.

The sense of the ultimate is a natural expression of the human spirit; for it is obvious that man has the unique freedom to stand outside and over even the most pressing tasks and preoccupations, and to survey the total plan of life to inquire after its total meaning, if any.

Today many people bear testimony to a revival of interest in these ultimate and searching questions. If this be true, it is not because our generation is more spiritual than former ones but because it is prompted to these more ultimate interests by several conditions which were not operative in the earlier part of the century. And perhaps these various conditions are but facets of one single crisis.

* Dr. Niebuhr is vice president of Union Theological Seminary and graduate professor of ethics and theology.

HUMAN INSECURITY

No matter how comfortable we may be in our jobs and no matter how complacent we may be about the operation of historical forces in our own nation, we are living in global insecurity and confronting the dread possibilities of an atomic conflict in global proportions. This situation alone is calculated to disturb our ease and to prompt some searching re-examination of the established presuppositions which have governed the life of our culture.

But even if this were not true, the course of our modern history has refuted so many of our working credos, and the rise of two successive tyrannies so similar and yet so different—Fascism and Communism—has created such a mood of doubt about our position in the whole mysterious drama of history, that every ultimate question which was assumed to be answered has been reopened.

Furthermore, our particular anxieties are but vividly expressed instances of the general condition in which we find ourselves. It is the condition of a wide hiatus between the technical efficiency of our culture and—so at least it seems—the confusion and crosspurposes of our human life.

This state of affairs must prompt questions which were supposed to have been answered confidently in the eighteenth and nineteenth centuries by the assurance that every human frustration and confusion was merely tentative and provisional, that they all would be solved when the historical progress of which everyone was certain would give men the power or the wisdom to overcome them. The disappointment of these hopes has created a cultural or spiritual crisis comparable to the political crisis occasioned by our global insecurity.

What is involved is the decay of the modern creed of progress and the perfectability of man, which has been the effective religion of modern man regardless of the form of his traditional religious loyalties.

UNREALISTIC SOLUTIONS

Several solutions have been proposed for the problems of this crisis. Let us look at them and weigh their adequacy.

Spiritual Values

One proposal which we hear frequently is the request for a new emphasis on spiritual values as contrasted with material interests. This answer may contain some truth, but the contrast between spiritual and material will certainly hide whatever truth it contains.

Spiritual values are conceived abstractly, as if they were something that could be added or subtracted from what we already have. Our problems obviously center around the question: How can we organize our common life with greater wisdom and charity; how can we live with a measure of serenity and patience amidst the perils and anxieties of our era? Such problems may be spiritual, but we do not solve them simply by devotion to abstractly conceived spiritual values.

Extension of Science

The second and by far the more popular proposal for solving our difficulties is that the "methods of science," which have served us so well in the conquest of nature, be extended to the human and historical scene, where they are supposed to function with the same efficacy as soon as the "cultural lag" between the natural and the historical sciences has been overcome. Usually the relative backwardness of the historical sciences is attributed to their comparative youth, a condition which time will cure.

There is a great deal of pathos in the projection of this hope, for it is but an expression of the very faith which has been discredited by history. It may be regarded as a last desperate effort to keep that faith alive. This is somewhat akin to the efforts of medieval monastics—Savonarola, for instance—to arrest the decay of the medieval order by a more rigorous application of monastic discipline. In both cases the radical challenge to the culture is not appreciated.

The idea that there is anything comparable between the management of nature and the management of historical processes is the basic illusion of a technical age. It is supported by the twin illusion that there is great similarity between the scientific knowledge of nature and the wisdom required for the solution of human problems. The differences are greater than the similarities, however grateful we have reason to be for whatever the social and psychological sciences have added to the wisdom by which we govern ourselves and each other.

There is a radical difference between the natural and the historical scene which makes it quite impossible to be scientific—with the same rigor of objectivity as the scientist in his observation of nature—in the judgments which we make of each other or of any common problem, each from his own perspective. This radical difference will exist, one may confidently predict, throughout human history. The "cultural lag," so-called, has nothing to do with it. The basis of the difference can be simply stated. It is that man is both an agent and an observer of the historical process; he is both a creator and a creature of that process.

REALITY OF MAN'S POSITION

This double position of man has all kinds of implications which practical men of affairs have had the wisdom to suspect, if not to affirm, while the academics have spun their theories about a new spirituality or a more rigorous science as the solution of our problems.

Human Dignity

Insofar as man is a creator and not merely a creature of any political process, he has a "dignity," the sense of which our culture has inherited from its Christian past. This dignity is outraged by plans to "manage" human nature as in certain modern social science projects, some of which come perilously near to the Marxist theories of the management of history—including the implicit or explicit corollary that some group of elite must do the managing.

Of course any wise leader of men knows either scientifically or intuitively (usually intuitively) how to achieve cooperation between men, how to realize uncoerced consent, or at least consent which requires a minimum of coercion. But the "science" of personnel management, to which modern business owes so much, has significantly incorporated wiser respect for the dignity of man than has been characteristic of more purely academic studies.

Self-Interest

The second consequence of the position of man as agent and as creature of any historical movement in which he is involved is that the recalcitrance of human self-interest in any common pursuit, economic *or* communal, must be taken for granted.

Included in this self-interest is a degree of ideological distortion in the judgments we make of each other. It is due to the fact that the observers and judges of any human scene are also interested agents of its procedures. Their stake in the proceedings naturally colors their judgments. It is this distortion which the historical and social scientists are inclined to attribute to remedial ignorance. Sometimes they ascribe it to particular causes. The Marxist error in attributing the corruption of interested judgment to an institution, namely the institution of property, and in hoping for its elimination through the abolition of property, is merely the most flagrant of many similar modern errors.

It is significant that men of affairs, whether in business or government, take the universality of some form of self-interest for granted, while academic wisdom looks toward its elimination. This is one of the many instances where practical wisdom agrees with the traditional religious analysis of the human situation and our official liberal culture challenges it. For our practical wisdom attests both to the universality of the taint and to its source in the self itself, and not in some subrational force in human nature which it is the function of a more disciplined reason to conquer.

Thus, while our learned men project vast schemes for the elimination of human "aggressiveness" as if it were merely a biological impulse, our common sense has long since recognized that we are dealing with the clash of individual and collective forms of interest, and that it is the task of wise statecraft, whether in business or government, to deflect, beguile, harness, and (in extreme instances) to suppress that interest.

The Christian Diagnosis

If this analysis is correct, the common sense which comes from common experience is more in agreement with the historic Hebraic and Christian interpretation of our human situation, including its estimate of both the dignity of man as creator and the misery of man as destroyer and sinner, than with the views which have been elaborated by modern culture. It is significant that these modern views have generated everywhere the euphoria of a soft utopianism, which is to be distinguished from the hard and dangerous utopianism of Communism but which evidently has its roots in similar errors.

In short, when we use our common sense, we are more "Christian" in the analysis of the human situation than when we apply our scientific theories. The question is whether the adequacy of the Christian diagnosis of the human situation, contrasted with the inadequacy of modern substitutes, will also persuade this generation to accept the Christian answer to the human problems of today.

THE CHRISTIAN ANSWER

It is characteristic of our contemporary problems that the readers of these pages will react to this suggestion with varying responses partly determined by the quality of the Christian faith with which they have been in contact.

Conceptual Distortions

It may be that some will be baffled or offended by the recommendation of this traditional solution of their problems because their conception of Christianity is colored by the individualistic and legalistic forms of it which are still prevalent and which will seem to be completely irrelevant to any serious problems of our life.

Others will be in touch with the more intellectual sections of the church, which have been anxious to make Christianity relevant to all modern problems. Unfortunately some of the typically "modern" churches have rather completely capitulated to the characteristic credos of our culture, so that they have given the impression that a "Christian" approach to any issue is the most "idealistic" possible solution which can be dreamed up.

The fact is that the confluence of perfectionist forms of Christianity and the utopianism of eighteenth-century rationalism have given our American culture its very particular flavor. And both our friends and our critics wonder what might be the hidden sources of the common sense by which we have managed, with tolerable skill, to bear the burdens of world hegemony and the complex problems of justice in a highly technical society.

The distortions of Christianity are significantly the fruits either of too desperate efforts to guard the unique truth of Christianity against modern culture or of too apologetic efforts to relate Christianity to the chracteristic credos of modern man. The consequence of this latter effort is to give Christian sanction to the utopian illusions which have infected our culture since the eighteenth century.

Mainstream of Faith

The proposition I wish to advance is that the best way of solving our "ultimate" questions is to return to the mainstream of Christian faith, whatever its momentary aberrations may be, for there are answers in its basic presuppositions which are superior to all the answers that we have got from modern substitutes.

The advocacy of such a faith does not include any particular interpretation of it and does not preclude the possibility that monstrous and dangerous errors may in fact be generated on the basis of Christian presuppositions. The assertion is merely that the total framework of meaning given in the Christian faith is more adequate for the solution of our problems than alternate frameworks.

Among these problems we may distinguish primarily two: (a) the problem of preserving the community on every level from the family to the potential world community, and (b) the problem of the individual as he stands beyond the destinies of his nation and civilization and inquires about the meaning of his existence.

PROBLEM OF THE COMMUNITY

The first problem, having to do with the creation of community and the establishment of justice, requires three presuppositions which have been frequently obscured in modern culture:

(1) Recognition must be given to the dignity of man which assures that in the ultimate instance he is regarded as an end in himself and

not merely as an instrument in a social or political process. (Liberal society has been inclined to emphasize this part of our Christian and Jewish inheritance—in contrast with modern totalitarianism which degrades man—though it may be questioned whether there is a very solid support in our culture for the idea of human dignity.)

(2) The law of love must be presupposed as the law of human existence.

(3) At the same time the perennial force of self-love and self-interest must be taken for granted.

Theories that substitute for man's self-interest some other ultimate principle of conduct (such as pure justice) are in danger of establishing *ad hoc* schemes of justice having their own validity in special situations but failing to deal adequately with the endless configurations of social life which man, in his freedom, is able to create above the level of pure nature. Systems of thought, whether Christian or secular, which do not accept the perennial force of individual or collective self-interest are simply irrelevant. They are the source of the various types of utopianism, soft and hard, harmless and dangerous, which our culture has generated.

Creative Harnessing

The persistence of self-interest requires that it be harnessed, transfigured, and rendered harmless by balancing competing self-interest against it.

A liberal society may pride itself on the fact that the free enterprise system which rests on the philosophy of Adam Smith has managed the creative harnessing of self-interest rather better than any alternative has. But right now we are in danger of becoming too complacent, just because the Marxist proposals for a managed economy have proved to be inadequate even in their mild democratic form, and positively demonic in their orthodox communist form.

Complacency is wrong and dangerous. The theory of free enterprise rests on an old "physiocratic" philosophy in which human history is nicely equated with nature and in which it is assumed that the balances of the community can be as simply achieved as are the balances of nature. But history is not so nice and simple. History distinguishes itself both by the fact of human freedom and by the essentially unlimited desires and ambitions of men.

As for human freedom, it makes simple proportions of power in the human community less balanced, and the balances less automatic, than is the case in nature. As for the essential inordinancy of all human desires, it insures that all disbalances are exploited by human ambition.

Therefore, justice demands not conformity to some abstract formula of justice but a tolerable harmony between competing forces.

Wider Obligation

This harmony is always partly contrived and partly automatic. The motive for its contrivance can be called the spirit of justice. It may also be defined as the spirit of love. In other words, it is a concern for, or sense of obligation to, a wider community than the one with which the self is immediately involved, whether that immediate community be the family, the business organization, or the nation.

The fact is that, while we must accept self-interest as a powerful force, particularly in its collective form, we cannot allow it as the basis for setting ethical standards. For we know that a too consistent self-interest actually destroys the self by cutting its creative contacts with the community, just as a too consistent doctrine of obedience to the national interest destroys that part of the national interest which is protected in the web of mutualities between friendly nations, the best current example of which is the common life of the free nations. In short, we must do more than harness self-interest; we must also provide a counterpull to it on every level:

The good administrator seeks to engage the self-interest of his workers and managers and at the same time to establish a degree of loyalty to the total enterprise.

The good statesman seeks to satisfy local interests and also to encourage loyalty to the nation.

In the international community we may expect any nation to protect its own interests, at least to the extent of not sacrificing them for the good of the whole; but this must not stop us from also seeking the point of concurrence between national and international interests.

On all these levels, formulas of justice must and will be devised to arbitrate conflicting interests. But they are not as important as the power of a wider interest, partly including and partly countering the narrower interest. In that sense it is love rather than justice which must solve the problems of human togetherness.

Accommodations for Harmony

Of course there must be all kinds of accommodations between competing interests for the sake of the harmony of the human community. But these accommodations are achieved not so much by fixed standards of equity as by the recognition on the part of each social force that the competing force is justified in its claim from its own perspective, just as our own claims are not so absolutely valid as we are tempted to regard them in the hour of competition. In other words, it is as important to recognize the creaturely limits of all men, including ourselves, as to recognize the dignity of man.

Democracy depends, in fact, as much on this plus of modesty in our relations as on any other factor. Democracy is a marvelous device for tolerating all kinds of interests and viewpoints, so long as they do not violate the minimal standards of justice and decency. Any simple moral fanaticism that assumes the absolute justice of a particular claim, or the absolute rightness of a particular viewpoint, is inimical to the community on any level; it is more frequently a peril than the more obvious forms of recalcitrance. Similarly, every good manager knows of the perils of fanatic claims in his organization and realizes that a single-minded devotion to a subordinate value may sow more confusion than any mere "criminal" activity.

Thus this whole matter reduces, again, to the proposition that men are both creative agents and creatures, and they become destroyers when in their creativity they refuse to acknowledge their creaturely limitations. A current ideological conflict in every modern technical society will point the moral:

There is a tension between two sections of the community consisting, on the one hand, of those who have their own security either in some special skill or their own economic strength and, on the other, of those who have no special skills and whose lives are exposed to the insecurities which arise from maladjustments in the whole economic process. The former prefer a society in which freedom and initiative are preserved; the latter prefer, if necessary, to sacrifice a degree of freedom for the sake of establishing minimal securities.

Democratic communities have long since decided that it is not feasible to sacrifice one set of values to the other. There is no rational resolution of these preferences because they spring out of the immediate interests of each class. But the debate continues on just how much or how little each set of values is to be emphasized. Democratic health requires not only that the debate be inconclusive but also that each class have a contrite awareness of the legitimacy of the other's preferences and of the interested character of its own.

This state of affairs must be regarded as symbolic of the requirement of love in the form of humility for the preservation of our common life.

PROBLEM OF THE INDIVIDUAL

Ultimately, however, the questions of the individual who rises in his freedom above the fate of his civilization and culture, and who perishes in the brevity of his life before even the most promising of his common enterprises can reach fulfillment, are more pressing religious questions than any which arise about how we can come to terms with our fellow men and establish a tolerable community with them.

The answers to these questions are more sheerly religious in the sense that any belief that there is a pattern of meaning beyond any which we are able to discern must justify itself, not by becoming a part of a general system of rational intelligibility, but by the recognition of the limits of reason in establishing meaning.

Key to Serenity

In these answers of faith we have the key to the possibility of living serenely in an age in which we can have no guaranteed security against the imagined and unimaginable perils of tomorrow.

We can discern a certain irony in the fact that a generation which looked so confidently into the future only yesterday, and which thought that it contained the promise of man's complete mastery of his own fate, should be reminded so forcefully today that man, for all his creative possibilities, is impotent to foresee or to control the larger pattern of the strange drama in which he plays a role so briefly. The humility of such a faith is very necessary, particularly for us as Americans who are so easily tempted to delusions of grandeur by our "incomparable" strength.

But the practical benefits arising from such a faith cannot propel us into it. It remains a faith, transcending reason. It is rational only in the sense that it is more reasonable than alternate faiths which result in despair today because yesterday they encouraged man to commit the primeval sin of thinking of himself more highly than he ought to think.

9.

Can the Businessman Apply Christianity?

BY HAROLD L. JOHNSON[*]

Some critics maintain that the fundamental religious tradition in this country—Judaeo-Christianity—is simply not applicable to the day-to-day problems of a business office. While these people may agree with the position taken by Thomas C. Campbell, Jr., in his discussion of "Capitalism and Christianity,"[1] to the effect that there is no inherent *conflict* between the values of religion and the values of an economic system, they claim that the individual businessman can find no *guidelines* in the specific doctrines on which most of our nation's religious creeds are based.

This may seem surprising in the face of what has been characterized as a "spiritual reawakening" in the United States today. After all, the United States is generally regarded as a Christian nation. Our coins declare "In God We Trust," and public school classes and even football games often open with prayer. Most Americans express some kind of belief in God; and if church membership is any evidence, the country surely should be classified as Christian. Over one hundred million of the population, or about 60 per cent of the total, are members of churches or synagogues. Furthermore, the percentage of the population with church mem-

[*] Mr. Johnson is associate professor of economics at Emory University. This article was written under a faculty research grant from the Bureau of Business and Economic Research, Georgia State College.

[1] *Harvard Business Review*, July-August 1957; also p. 165 of this volume.

bership has risen to the highest on record in the postwar "return" to religion.

Nevertheless, as one study indicates, "religion plays little part, or at least at the conscious level, in the decisions" made by individuals;[2] and many churchgoers seem unaware of the relevance of their religion to the problems and decisions which confront them daily. Similarly, students of American business in analyzing the "American business creed" have concluded that "the creed bows to the importance of religion, admits seeking religious guidance, but continues to be a predominantly secular ideology."[3]

OPERATING GUIDE

To my mind, this is most unfortunate because Christian doctrines do, in fact, offer a perspective from which to view modern commercial life, and this perspective *can make a difference* in the decisions and actions of businessmen. They are relevant in that they can help him choose the "best" (not necessarily the "correct") alternative in a given situation. Some theologians call this the "always dramatic interaction between God and man," while an occasional businessman points out that religion is not just a Sunday matter but an operating guide in the complexities of daily living.[4]

I want to demonstrate this point by taking several basic articles of doctrine and relating them to business life. In doing so, I shall reflect my own experience and my own convictions, but many of the ideas expressed stem from the thinking and discussion in which I participated at a two-week seminar at the Harvard Business School. Here, under the sponsorship of the Danforth Foundation, businessmen, educators, and religious leaders are brought together for the specific purpose of tackling business-religious problems on the realistic basis of actual case situations. To me, just this demonstration of the fact that men feel the need to increase understanding in this area is itself of the highest significance.

[2] Marquis W. Childs and Douglass Cater, *Ethics in a Business Society* (New York, New American Library of World Literature, 1954), pp. 173-174.

[3] Francis X. Sutton et al., *The American Business Creed* (Cambridge, Harvard University Press, 1956), p. 269.

[4] See O. A. Ohmann, " 'Skyhooks' (With Special Implications for Monday Through Friday)," *Harvard Business Review*, May-June 1955, p. 33; also p. 70 of this volume.

No Clear Blueprint

The application of religion's ultimate insights to specific situations is, of course, a tremendously difficult task. There are no blueprints, no simple rules to go by. Christianity does not present the executive with a tool kit of easy-to-use rules and precepts by which problems can be solved. The doctrines are not bound up in a simple list of "dos" and "don'ts" somewhat in the style of a book of etiquette, which if followed will result in harmonious, gentlemanly relations within and without a business.

But it does offer a *frame of reference,* a universe view, which instead of giving peace of mind and easy success in human relations often breaches the barricade of self-assurance, focuses on difficulties, and erases naïve hopes of business progress ever onward, ever upward.

This frame of reference is constructed from specific Christian ideas. Accordingly, let us look at several of these articles of doctrine—the concepts of God, creation, man, sin, forgiveness, and Christian vocation—and indicate how each furnishes insights into problems and actions confronting businessmen.

THE CONCEPT OF GOD

One of the distinguishing features of Western civilization is belief in the order and plan of the universe, which comes, Christians and Jews affirm, from God. But what other factors enter into the Judaeo-Christian understanding of the nature and character of the Supreme Being? While mystery shrouds this question, so that we "see only darkly," most of us in some sense agree that God is a personal, transcendent Being whose nature is revealed to us in the life of Jesus.

The words *personal* and *Being* are extremely significant, for they are used to imply, not an anthropomorphic concept, but rather that God is closely connected with human life. They mean that God exists, not as a process working through history—though God does work in history—but as a reality that *cares for* and *is concerned about* the past, present, and future of human existence. The God of Christian and Jew is an Almighty Father who exists and who loves all his children with a divine passion: "Praise the

Lord, all nations! . . . For great is his steadfast love toward us; and the faithfulness of the Lord endures forever."[5]

God is also transcendent. He is the Absolute, above and beyond human processes and problems. "With men it is impossible, but not with God; for all things are possible with God."[6] As the Supreme Reality, God stands at the center of existence, the Ultimate by which all things are judged and evaluated.

Temperature Test

But what is the significance of these observations concerning God for the businessman? Very simply, they place everything human under the rule of God, warning against the idolatry of putting the business firm, the nation, "free private enterprise," or the career at the center of life. With such a perspective, all things pertaining to business stand under the judgment of God as *limited* goals and loyalties.

If, however, we accept the definition of religion as "man's profoundest solicitude about the things he counts most valuable,"[7] then in all honesty it must be stated that for many businessmen the worship of God is not the center or focus of their religion. According to one leading churchman, the "god" of an individual can be determined by the use of a "temperature test"; that is, *the* concept, goal, or loyalty which gets people most excited, wrought up, and agitated is *their* "Supreme Being."[8] Application of such a test undoubtedly would reveal a variety of personal idols for business executives: the enterprises for which they have labored for years, the economic order which has given them and their nation so much in material goods, or the goal of becoming the most noted men in their industries.

Many investigators have testified to the company-centered frame of reference so common among executives today. As Howard R. Bowen has put it in his *Social Responsibilities of the Businessman:*

[5] Psalms 117. (All scriptural citations will be from the Revised Standard Version of the *Holy Bible* unless otherwise noted.)

[6] Mark 10:27.

[7] Ralph Barton Perry, quoted in Alexander Miller, *The Renewal of Man* (Garden City, New York, Doubleday & Company, Inc., 1955), p. 43.

[8] James Luther Adams, "A Faith for Free Men," *Together We Advance,* edited by S. H. Fritchman (Boston, The Beacon Press, 1946), pp. 45-65.

It [the corporation] is an object which has needs and aspirations, which experiences many of the vicissitudes of life, and to which one can give selfless devotion and unswerving loyalty. Moreover, the manager thinks of the corporation as having a kind of immortality in that it goes on—or should go on—indefinitely into the future. He thinks of his own leadership of it as temporary. One of his deepest concerns is to see that it prospers under his care. . . . This description of the manager's attitude suggests an almost mystical relationship between him and the corporation.[9]

With the Judaeo-Christian view of God, the totality of individual *and social or institutional* existence comes under judgment and evaluation. Even the economic system of "free business enterprise"—or any other economic order for that matter—falls under the scrutiny and creative criticism of a Biblical perspective. This questioning of "free enterprise" is particularly pertinent for these times, for while some businessmen appear to put the corporation at the center of their personal faith, others seem to worship the economic system. Their creed embraces a complex of beliefs, which laud individualism, private property, competition, and a relatively laissez-faire economic order. Judging by the temperature test, the "devils" of this creed are high taxes, government encroachment, and creeping socialism.

Faith in the corporation, in one's career, or in free enterprise, of course, is no more clearly antireligious than the Communists' fanatical abjuration of everything except materialism. Both are idolatrous; both commit the fundamental sin of the Judaeo-Christian faith—putting man and man's values in the place of God.

Needless to say, businessmen are not the only individuals ignoring the Biblical admonition, "Thou shalt have no other gods before me"; for self-centeredness is a universal human characteristic.

All of us, then, must answer the same dread question: "What has *first* priority for me?" or "In this particular pricing or personnel or financing decision, what is my *ultimate* criterion—my own career, the enterprise, the system, or what?" The Christian concept of God provides real help as we formulate a reply.

[9] New York, Harper & Brothers, 1953, p. 87.

THE DOCTRINE OF CREATION

The doctrine of creation is of profound interest, for it supports the position that God may be found in the issues and problems of economic life. According to the writer of Genesis, "In the beginning God created the heavens *and the earth*. . . . And God saw everything that he had made, and behold, it was very good."[10] The Biblical view of creation, then, is not that things of the spirit or of heaven are "good" while material things are "evil," as in the thinking of ascetic mysticism. There is not a gulf between things of the spirit or of God and the world which He created. God, on the contrary, created *both* heaven and earth and found *both* good. Furthermore, according to the Scriptures, God instructed man to subdue the earth and to have dominion over it.[11]

The Christian perspective, then, does not treat material goods and services—the peculiar domain of the businessman—as inherently evil and sinful. In fact, God gave specific instructions to man for the use and development of goods and services.

Many religious critics, however, have couched their onslaught against a business civilization in the terms of antimaterialism, implying that religious and spiritual values are somehow incompatible with new automobiles, television sets, and fresh-frozen lobster claws.[12] Even businessmen seem often to feel that because they deal particularly with the material, worldly goods of this life, *ipso facto* they fall short of the Kingdom of God. But, as Alexander Miller makes abundantly clear, Christianity and Judaism are not world-renouncing religions. He states:

[There is in the Hebrew attitude] . . . a lip-smacking, exuberant delight in the ingenious beauty and variety of the created world; in wine and milk, olive-oil and honey. It is a world whose paths drop fatness, where the little hills rejoice on every side. Such a world has a place for heroism, but none for asceticism.[13]

Corporation executives are counseled, consequently, by the doctrine of creation that they are doing work which does not inevitably have the taint of sin—that in their production, pricing,

[10] Genesis 1:1, 31 (italics added).
[11] Genesis 1:28.
[12] See J. D. Glover, *The Attack on Big Business* (Boston, Division of Research, Harvard Business School, 1954).
[13] *Op. cit.*, p. 54.

and sales decisions they *may* be doing the will of God.

Another aspect of the doctrine of creation which is significant for Christian executives is the concept of stewardship. As a matter of fact, "the most radical theory" of property known stems from the Christian view of creation.[14] According to this view man owns nothing. As presented in an official National Council of Churches statement, "All resources of the earth . . . are gifts of God . . . and God is the only absolute owner."[15] The "temporal owner" of labor, capital, or natural resources, accordingly, is a trustee or steward of such property for God and for his fellow man. The businessman, while given rights and powers to use resources by earthly laws of contract and sales, is responsible to others for the actions and policies of the enterprise which he helps administer.

This concept of Christian stewardship provides part of the religious underpinnings for the philosophy of "social responsibility" that many businessmen espouse. This approach to business affairs requires managers to weigh the impact of their policies on the many interest groups, including the community at large, which are affected by the enterprise. The stewardship concept ties this "balancing of interests" to responsibility to God and, as a consequence of that responsibility, also to fellow man.

THE NATURE OF MAN

The nature of man as postulated by Christian doctrine is highly relevant to the problems of the administrator. According to Christian tradition, man is a complex of conflicting, opposing attributes. He is capable of approaching the infinite; yet he is sinful. He is created in the image of God; yet he is inherently imperfect. Jehovah and Satan both are part of his being. Let us look first at the Godlike side.

Man the Angel

The Genesis story tells us that "God created man in his own image, in the image of God he created him."[16] The story makes

---

[14] Quoted from the commentary by F. Ernest Johnson in Howard R. Bowen, *op. cit.*, p. 244.

[15] *Christian Principles and Assumptions for Economic Life*, statement adopted by the General Board of the National Council of the Churches of Christ in the U.S.A., September 15, 1954 (New York, 1954), p. 2.

[16] Genesis 1:27.

clear, in addition, that man is worthy—and able—to commune and converse with God. The whole flow of the Scriptures emphasizes this close linkage between human beings and Ultimate Reality. The significance of man in Christian belief is, perhaps, best typified in the famous Old Testament song:

When I look at thy heavens, the work of thy fingers, and the moon and the stars which thou hast established; what is man that thou art mindful of him, and the son of man that thou dost care for him? *Yet thou hast made him little less than God,* and dost crown him with glory and honor. Thou hast given him dominion over the works of thy hands.[17]

Thus one side of the Christian view of man declares that man is full of dignity and able to do extraordinary things, even though he is a finite being. As one writer states:

Man, in the Christian view, has not been placed in the universe as one thing among other things. He is not, for weal or woe, installed in a ready-made world; he co-operates in its genesis.[18]

But what significance does this observation have for the businessman of today? It suggests that the real explanation for the remarkable modern developments in science, technology, and administration lies in the fact that God made men able to exert such force in the universe. This view suggests, more specifically, that men have been equipped with the physical, intellectual, and moral capacities for solving the involved economic and business problems that face them.

How often do we stand appalled at the size of the task which confronts us? And how frequently does our very anxiety about our competence to handle it—alone or in cooperation with others —weaken or even wash out our efforts? Braced by an innate confidence in the power of human beings, and therefore in our own power, we can face complex decisions boldly and make them effectively.

Further, a basic confidence in our fellow man, coupled with a continuing effort to judge just where his greatest competencies lie, provides a frame of reference for personnel decisions. Execu-

[17] Psalms 8:3-6 (italics added).
[18] J. H. Oldham, *Work in Modern Society* (New York, Morehouse-Gorham Co., Inc., 1950), p. 36.

tives are constantly called on to take gambles in situations where a man must be chosen to do a job. It is helpful to have a guideline: "Play it safe; do not trust the man," or "Believe in him, and he will measure up." Christian doctrine urges us to err on the side of confidence, not mistrust. As Donald K. David, former dean of the Harvard Business School, has observed:

> Without delegation so extensive that it involves real risk—the placing of bets on people's ability—individuals in an organization cannot develop the competence which makes delegation possible. We begin to believe that delegation better serves its purpose when we take chances on subordinates than when we hesitate for fear they will fall short.[19]

Finally, confidence in his fellows encourages a man to make vast concessions of personal pride and status in his effort to understand another's viewpoint. Needless to say, this does not involve the obligation to agree with his antagonist; indeed, the clearer his understanding grows, the more he may disagree. However, the thrust of his effort will be to understand, to consider, and to judge fairly.

Man the Devil

The Christian understanding of man does not end, however, with a being possessing tremendous creative capacities; it goes on to encompass a being with an inevitable tendency "to sin and fall short of the glory of God."

For the Christian, sin is the "moral evil that lies at the juncture of nature and Spirit."[20] This is not the black-and-white perspective, referred to above, which summarily tags all material matters evil and all spiritual things divine; nor is it equivalent to the oft-stated modern idea that there is no sin. In some current ideology, all the difficulties and calamities of the world are said to arise simply from ignorance or misshapen institutions. This modern rationale optimistically contends that all problems can be removed by education, moralizing, or revisions in the institutional framework of society.

[19] Edward C. Bursk, Editor, *The Management Team* (Cambridge, Harvard University Press, 1954), p. 4.
[20] Reinhold Niebuhr, *An Interpretation of Christian Ethics* (New York, Meridian Books, Inc., 1956), p. 81.

The dualistic viewpoint offers no hope whatever for those of us who are involved deeply in the material aspect of living. The Christian view, on the other hand, places sin at the spiritual core of man. In Reinhold Niebuhr's words:

> But man is destined, both by the imperfections of his knowledge and by his desire to overcome his finiteness, to make absolute claims for his partial and finite values. He tries, in short, to make himself God.[21]

This Christian admission that man is sinful, and inevitably trying to puff up his own importance, serves as a warning to ambitious executives who are advancing through the hierarchy of an industrial organization to positions of responsibility and prestige. Almost inevitably, such individuals will assume exaggerated views of their abilities, judgments, and contributions to the enterprise of which they are a part. These inflated self-appraisals may be a particular occupational disease of men in positions of responsibility, and cannot help but affect their behavior and their decision making.

But the doctrine of sin issues a warning to managers at all levels that their self-interest and pride are often woven into the fabrics of their judgments and policies even though they may firmly believe their policies to be objective and impartial:

> Plant managers may suggest a program of expansion and modernization, characterizing it as essential for company health, when the strength of their interest actually stems from their desire to enlarge their own areas of control.

> Other company executives may stress that their "socially responsible" philosophy works to the general benefit; yet basically such a philosophy may be a subtle device to maintain economic power in their own hands by extending their influence and decision-making power into so many nonbusiness areas that they become benevolent dictators.

> Other managers may support mammoth advertising expenditures and rapid model changes as "in the public interest" since they foster a high level of employment and national income, while the real objective may be to reduce competition and increase company net revenue.

> Corporations may give funds to charitable or educational institutions and may argue for them as great humanitarian deeds, when in fact they are simply trying to buy community good will.

[21] *Ibid.*, p. 82.

A Clouded Future

The concept of sin, furthermore, cautions against an easy optimism that business enterprises are going to solve all their problems, establishing "big happy families" of employees, employers, consumers, and suppliers. Failures, mistakes, and antagonisms, according to a Christian calculation, will always characterize company operations despite "human relations" or "social responsibility" or "professional management," or any other expanding concept. Of course, new ways of looking at and doing things may lessen tensions and reduce problems to more manageable proportions. But no manager should expect, even subconsciously, that they will give him a problemless world.

The excessive optimism of many business executives crops up in the widely held, somewhat mystical, belief that free enterprise, if left alone, will build a "heavenly city" on earth and produce a steadily expanding standard of living for all. By the same token, some businessmen talk as though each American family will have three cars in every garage, color television, electronic cooking, and a helicopter in the back yard if only it will accept, unchallenged, "sensible business leadership." And indeed there seems to be a considerable amount of evidence to support this point of view. The Christian concept of man, however, balances these calculations of progress "ever onward" with the warning that incomplete knowledge, self-centeredness, and faulty institutional patterns mean that the future, though it can be better than the present, holds continued conflict, problems, and stupidity.

Finally, the businessman who understands the doctrine of sin will not be so shocked and self-righteous when he perceives the "taint of corruption" in others, because he will know it exists in his own heart as well. He will be less resentful of the checks and balances against his own power, economic and otherwise, in modern society and will accept the need for "countervailing power," competition, or government action to help him keep his own company in line. He will be cautious about attacking the other party in labor negotiations as "selfish" or "hypocritical," because he will be conscious of these same weaknesses in his position. Incidentally, if more controversies with unions were carried out in that way, we might not usher in a new era of brotherly love, but tensions would be lowered and solutions more easily found.

THE DOCTRINE OF FORGIVENESS

The Biblical picture of man as a creature of basic contradictions means that he will inevitably sin and cannot, by his own efforts, keep himself from so doing. Alone, human beings are unable to cure this disease of the spirit. As Alexander Miller states, "The human dilemma . . . calls not for a resolve but for a rescue."[22]

The Christian believes that this rescue is effected by the forgiving love of God as witnessed in the life and death of Jesus Christ. "But God shows his love for us in that while we were yet sinners Christ died for us."[23] The doctrine of forgiveness also suggests that, as God forgives human beings, so should they forgive one another. But not everyone can forgive; the gift can be given only by—

. . . those who know that they are not good, who feel themselves in need of divine mercy, who live in a dimension deeper and higher than that of moral idealism, feel themselves as well as their fellow man convicted of sin by a holy God and know that the differences between the good man and bad man are insignificant in his sight.[24]

The concept of forgiveness has many applications for the business manager beyond the obvious one of overlooking or forgetting the errors and slights of others which are so much a part of the business day.

It provides a constant reminder that men cannot be expected to make basic changes in their methods and attitudes without help from the outside. It does little good to tell a subordinate, "You simply *must* be more careful about the figures in your reports"; part of the executive's task is to help the man improve, by training, by closer supervision, or even—if the situation seems hopeless and yet the man is too valuable to lose—by moving him over into a job that he can handle.

Faith and hope in divine forgiveness offer an additional insight

[22] *Op. cit.,* p. 59.
[23] Romans 5:8.
[24] Reinhold Niebuhr, *op. cit.,* pp. 203-204.

to businessmen in the throes of decision making. How often managers have to devise solutions to problems with only incomplete and often erroneous data available! How often an administrator is all too conscious of conflicting goals and of conflicting group interests!

Even with today's advanced analytical tools, uncertainty remains a basic characteristic of business operations. Furthermore, moral dilemmas cannot be fed into an electronic data-processing machine; in many situations all the available alternatives seem to have serious ethical deficiencies which do not yield to a slide rule. For example:

In deciding whether to lay off a portion of a labor force, managers are acutely aware that keeping the men employed may endanger the financial health of the entire organization, jeopardizing the economic interests of customers, suppliers, other employees, stockholders, and the community at large. At the same time, they well appreciate the hardships that will be visited on the men who are let go.

In the presentation of information about a product for advertising purposes, executives may be concerned about statements which are factually or legally correct but are designed to mislead the potential customer and stimulate him to think something which is not true. Company officials may fear, on the other hand, that if such advertising practices are not used, revenues will decline to the point where many individuals depending on the sales success of the company are likely to suffer.

Thus, businessmen contend constantly with problems in which every available proposal is obviously less than perfect. In these circumstances, the concept of a forgiving God is sorely needed. As Miller states:

And since our grasp of the faith is always unsure and our mastery of the facts always partial and limited; since we can neither assess our motives with confidence nor calculate consequences with certainty, we are cast in the end always on the forbearance and forgivness of God.[25]

Administrators and other men of decision consequently find the doctrine of forgiveness a peculiar blessing. While reliance on a forbearing Ultimate to pardon faulty human actions easily can

[25] *Op. cit.*, p. 101.

serve as a rationalization for shallow, selfish decisions, it does give men the courage to attempt the formation and execution of policies about complex matters. The alternatives to this approach to problem solving are twofold: (1) businessmen can withdraw from points of decision—which is impossible, after all, for they cannot abdicate altogether from the human race; or (2) they can cynically ignore their spiritual deficiencies, shortages of information, and conflicting goals, and use their power to make their decisions stick. Neither of these alternatives is a live option for managers imbued with a Christian outlook on life.

CHRISTIAN VOCATION

The doctrine of Christian vocation is based on the "call" issued to man by a forgiving and merciful God "to repentance and faith and to a life of fellowship and service in the Church."[26] It is a call to rebirth and transformation, assuring mortals that the Ultimate will accept them into His kingdom and save them from the self-centeredness of mortal perspectives and motivations. "Behold, your God will come with vengeance with the recompense of God. He will come and save you."[27] "[God] saved us and called us with a holy calling, not in virtue of our works but in virtue of his own purpose and the grace which he gave us in Christ Jesus."[28]

While this summons to salvation may have otherworldly implications, it is clearly a challenge to change in orientation and attitude here and now. "The kingdom of God is not coming with visible display, and so people will not say, 'Look! Here it is,' nor 'There it is,' for the kingdom of God is within you."[29] It is clear, furthermore, that the call is not to any particular occupational position such as sales manager, plumber, or accountant, but rather to a personal revolution which puts God at the center of existence:

The Bible knows no instance of a man's being called to an earthly profession or trade by God. St. Paul, for example, is called by God to be an apostle, he is not "called" to be a tent-maker. . . .

[26] Alan Richardson, *The Biblical Doctrine of Work* (London, Student Christian Movement Press, Ltd., 1952), p. 35.

[27] Isaiah 35:4.

[28] II Timothy 1:9.

[29] Luke 17:20-21, *The New Testament, A Private Translation in the Language of the People*, translated by Charles B. Williams (Chicago, Moody Press, 1949).

We cannot with propriety speak of God's calling a man to be an engineer or a doctor or a schoolmaster. God calls doctors and engineers and schoolmasters to be prophets, evangelists, pastors and teachers as laymen in His Church. . . .[30]

The first aspect, then, of a conception of Christian vocation is a sense of reformation of "one's whole heart and mind and soul into a new relationship with God who continually seeks us out."[31]

With rebirth as a saved person, according to the Christian, comes a tremendous sense of gratitude and, consequently, a sense of responsibility to God for this salvation. Miller describes this aspect of the doctrine of Christian vocation as follows:

The man who acknowledges himself debtor to God is committed to serve him in the midst of the world. He accepts a new *Stand*—a new status of responsibility—in relation to other men. He is not only called into the community of God's debtors, but he is called to serve God in the total community of mankind. . . . He may be at once a church official, citizen, a cobbler, and the father of a family. This matrix of obligation defines the form of his earthly vocation as it derives from his heavenly citizenship, his status as a forgiven sinner.[32]

Thus while the Christian is not called to be a cobbler or a corporation vice president, the free gift of the Kingdom of God prompts gratitude and responsibility, which overflow into his "earthly" work as a citizen, company official, and father. The impact of the call to God's kingdom is felt thereby in the social, political, and economic relationships in which he lives.

A second meaningful feature of the doctrine of vocation relates to work as the divine ordinance for man. Before "the fall of man into sin," according to the Genesis story, man was to "fill the earth and subdue it; and . . . have dominion over . . . every living thing that moves upon the earth."[33] Man was put in the Garden of Eden "to till it and keep it."[34] As Richardson notes, Biblical writers expound "the notion of man's ordinary, everyday, routine

[30] Alan Richardson, *op. cit.*, pp. 35, 36.
[31] Albert Terril Rasmussen, *Christian Social Ethics* (New York, Prentice-Hall, Inc., 1956), p. 266.
[32] *Op. cit.*, p. 148.
[33] Genesis 1:28.
[34] Genesis 2:15.

labour" as "the normal, fitting and inevitable lot of mankind."[35] Richardson concludes, "The teaching of the Old Testament on the subject of work may be generally summed by saying that it is a necessary and indeed God-appointed function of human life."[36]

The two Reformation thinkers, Luther and Calvin, further emphasize the importance of work, stressing that even mundane labor may be a place for service to God and man. Luther agreed, "a cobbler, a smith, and a farmer, each has the work of his trade, yet they are all alike consecrated priests and bishops."[37] Rasmussen in summarizing the Reformation contribution to the doctrine states that "all work—worthy of doing at all—is a responsible ministry, elevated to an ordination of service to God and to neighbor."[38]

How does this idea of Christian vocation apply to the executive? There are many ways; here are some of them:

1. The concept of vocation imposes a special set of motivations on business managers. Service to God and consequently service to the many individuals affected by the enterprise is the Christian mainspring of action, rather than accumulations of status, prestige, dollars, or power.

Since one task is as important as another from the Christian viewpoint of vocation, the businessman is obligated to respect the work of factory, mine, and office, as well as his own function. Further, he should make an effort to endow it with dignity and social usefulness.

The social necessity of many executive positions is readily apparent to most observers, for the coordination, management, and planning of enterprise forms an essential part of large-scale industrial operations. But a similar sense of dignity and importance is usually denied to those who work on small parts of a productive process, tabulating figures in a ledger or performing a single act on an assembly line.

The doctrine of vocation implies, then, that the business manager has the responsibility to show individuals the worthwhileness of their labor. And, further, he ought to be actively concerned about upgrading it, making it more interesting, providing the maximum opportunities for personal fulfillment both in the job itself and in the work environment.

2. It raises disturbing questions about some types of business activity which, perhaps, cannot qualify as work consecrated to God and to fellow

[35] *Op. cit.*, p. 21.
[36] *Ibid.*, p. 23.
[37] Martin Luther, quoted in Albert Terril Rasmussen, *op. cit.*, p. 267.
[38] *Op. cit.*, p. 268.

man. The element of dignity and social utility of labor may be difficult to uncover in some types of advertising, for instance, which are based on the assumption that human beings are stupid and gullible. Advertising stressing "extraordinary" differences between brands of gasoline or of cigarettes in the face of laboratory evidence that such differences do not exist hardly comes under the heading of social usefulness. Advertising practices and rapid model obsolescence which accentuate acquisitive and conspicuous consumption tendencies of Americans, likewise, may not qualify as important work, even though such practices may be cloaked in arguments about the "public interest."

3. Still another implication from this doctrine of Christian vocation strikes one with real force: God cares not whether a man is an executive or a laborer. His primary concern is with what *kind* of man he is, on and off the job. Does he let his business so absorb him that he is no longer a father, a friend, or a citizen? Does he treat people as human beings, or building blocks? Does he brush aside the ordinary standards of courtesy because he is "too busy to think about that kind of thing"? Maybe he can accept the excuse that "my job is so important—everything else will have to be secondary." Maybe even his family and friends will say, "Well, that's just the way he is, and, after all, he is so talented that it's all right." But the doctrine of Christian vocation raises real questions as to whether God uses these same scales.

Conclusion

As stated at the outset, the task of this discussion is to demonstrate that there can be important connections between Christian concepts and the activities of business enterprise. Christianity, it seems to me, offers a most fruitful frame of reference by which to view the realities of business activities. Executives equipped with such a perspective do many things differently from those not so equipped; a major difference between a Christian and a non-Christian approach, as many writers have noted, is a difference in attitude and depth of understanding in confronting all the perplexities of business affairs.

Businessmen holding this viewpoint would, for example, be less likely to commit the idolatry of worshiping the business enterprise, economic system, or career as the ultimate of existence. Thoroughgoing humility rising out of a realization of one's grievous shortcomings, balanced by freedom from anxiety stemming from an awareness of judgment *and forgiveness* by a Being beyond the level of man, would also characterize the Christian administrator.

One point should be made in this connection: the Judaeo-Christian outlook is made up of a network of interrelated doctrines. One concept is insufficient without the support of the others. The doctrine of man as the image of God without the concept of God offers an exaggerated understanding of the capabilities of man; and the idea of sin without forgiveness would make business excutives either cynics or prime candidates for mental institutions.

This interlocking set of beliefs, though not a formal code of laws, offers the businessman an attitude, a way of looking at the world and its problems, a set of values which can be far more revolutionary in its effects than any blueprint for an institution or daily calendar of business activities.

If the business manager will rid himself of the notion that the doctrines of the church—any church—offer him nothing but vague ideas about human relationships, and sit down with the theologian to explore the teachings of his faith, he will find vast quantities of material out of which he can construct a map for his business life. If he takes the time and trouble to probe such apparently abstract ideas as the nature of God and man, the doctrines of forgiveness, sin, and creation, he will find them rich in implications and applications.

Working in concert with theologians, and perhaps collegiate schools of business (both cooperatively and separately), he can make ever more clear and more concrete the relevance of a Judaeo-Christian perspective to business administration.

10.

Capitalism and Chrisitanity

By Thomas C. Campbell, Jr.*

Few theologians understand the fundamental goals of our free enterprise system, and economists are rarely inclined to try to explain capitalism in the light of religious principles. An even greater gap is left between the pursuits of individual enterprisers and the basic objectives of religion. Consequently, more often than not, these businessmen who are such great contributors to the progress of our society wonder whether the economic system they serve is not, after all, really antireligious.

What is the result of this suppressed but gnawing doubt? For one thing, many businessmen are troubled by a pessimism—an unusual emotion for most executives—or even a feeling of defensiveness when faced with the question of whether their work is truly Christian (in the broad sense of the whole Judaeo-Christian tradition). This distresses them; they wish to live and work in harmony with their religious beliefs, but they are constantly faced with the realities of a business world which demands certain actions commonly considered out of harmony with recognized religious goals.

Faced with this dilemma, businessmen are likely to take refuge in statements like, "Let's not mix religion with business"; or else they go to the other extreme of trying to equate the two, of

* Mr. Campbell is assistant dean of the College of Commerce and associate professor of economics at West Virginia University.

seeking to prove to themselves—and others—that the practices and objectives of business and the church are identical. Neither way out of the problem is satisfying or satisfactory:

Any thoughtful man interested in organized religion knows that religious ethics and religious living cannot be applied at certain times and places, only to be ignored at others. If such a "religion" does exist, it must be empty of content and meaning, for it will be observed only when convenient. A set of principles which are marked "For Sunday Only" is no religion at all.

On the other hand, it is unrealistic to claim that religion and business are essentially the same thing—that their goals, practices, and personnel are interchangeable. Each has its own role, each is a separate part of a whole. It would be equally useless to try to "prove" that the goals of a plumber and a painter are the same—though they may indeed have some common ends—and it would be equally unnecessary. To say the two are different is not to set them apart or put one above the other on some ultimate scale of values. It simply recognizes the bewildering variety of man's pursuits, talents, and objectives.

I do not think businessmen want to ignore this problem, as the easy alternative to forever doubting the worthiness of their chosen profession. So let us meet the issue head-on, and consider whether or not our capitalistic system is inherently or inevitably in conflict with religious goals and requirements. With this basic issue clarified, it will be far easier for each one of us to work out a system of values, as businessmen, which are both acceptable in a religious sense and practical as guides to our day-to-day professional lives.

CHURCH AND OFFICE

I do not believe that our capitalistic system is "bad," or that it cannot be reconciled with religion, as I shall indicate. But, unfortunately, many businessmen do not seem to agree with me, judging by their prevailing attitudes.

It is true, of course, that many businessmen are active workers in the religious institutions of the United States. They make financial and other contributions to the churches. By generally accepted standards of comparison, they are religious people. Yet these men, too, spend the greater part of their working hours in business, and in so doing make every reasonable attempt to meet competition and operate successfully as do their fellow business-men who do not take an active part in organized religion.

The point is that business activity takes place on five or six days in the week while religious work is confined to Sundays and occasional evenings. It is not a common practice to engage in religious discussion or religious activity during the so-called work-ing hours of the business day, and most businessmen make a sharp division between their church and their office. They com-monly avoid any reference to the one when engaged in the other; seldom do they breach the wall they have built between the two.

As a matter of fact, many of them doggedly insist that the two must remain separate. Their contention is that efforts by clergy-men, businessmen, or professional economists to consider the two at the same time do more harm than good, and that religious goals are in their place only when expounded by the clergy and by laymen while they are engaged exclusively in religious work. They further contend that economic goals are distinctly different from religious goals, which are by their very nature impractical and out of line with reality. This point of view is well illustrated by Josephus Daniels:

> The pew wishes sermons that are redolent of the whole Gospel. They tire of essays, discussions on economics, solutions to social problems, and the like. They have a surfeit of these on weekdays. . . .[1]

Continuing Debate

Following this line of reasoning, much of the early criticism of Christian churches in the United States involved the question of whether religious groups should take any official position in regard to activities of organized labor and the attitudes of many industrial-ists toward organized labor. The question of church participation in social problems was debated vigorously by such well-known clergymen as Henry Ward Beecher and Washington Gladden, and covered extensively in articles and editorials of religious publica-tions. This question has not been and probably never can be com-pletely settled. The dispute still continues. Thus:

[1] Quoted in Frank H. Knight and Thornton W. Marriam, *The Economic Order and Religion* (New York, Harper & Brothers, 1947), p. 129.

In recent years, the work of the Department of the Church and Economic Life of the National Council of Churches has uncovered—and unleashed—considerable disagreement as to whether the church should take any part in studying economic problems. A series of books published on *Ethics and Economics of Society* has been part of a major effort in this field, but it has met with vigorous criticism. Even those who have been otherwise active with the National Council could not agree on the advisability of sponsoring studies of this nature. Other organizations, too—like the American Council of Christian Laymen—have strongly opposed these studies.

This determined effort on the part of businessmen to divide God from Caesar both reinforces and gains strength from the idea that the two are irreconcilable. If we insist that the two "do not mix," we are driven to the assumption that one is good, and the other bad—that they are irreconcilable because they are out of harmony with each other, and that they are out of harmony because our economic system does not measure up to the standards and demands of our religion.

So the argument inevitably runs, and it leads straight to many of the attacks on our enterprise system which businessmen so deplore. Unless they join hands with the theologians and face up to the issues involved, the religiously based criticisms of which they complain—and many of the political criticisms as well—will continue to flourish. By ducking the tough ones, by subscribing to the idea that "business and religion don't mix," by telling the church to "tend to its own affairs," they perpetuate the notion that religion and capitalism are in conflict. On this assumed conflict rest many of the modern attacks on our enterprise system.

Four Common Accusations

Let us now look at four of the more common misconceptions and traditional accusations which confuse the relationship between religion and business and tend to divide the two, setting one against the other.

"The Scriptures Are No Help"

Possibly the first on the list is that "religious teachings just are not designed to apply to economic systems; they have no contribution to make, because they are concerned with a totally different phase of life." Anyone who takes this position overlooks the fact that all our basic religious teachings and philosophies are several centuries old. By comparison, our business system is extremely new. The illustrations used in early religious writings—the applications of fundamental teachings—were based on events and circumstances at the time in which the writings took place. The messages or principles involved are not necessarily dated or limited to the time of their origin; in fact, many of the messages apply to all times with absolutely no limit. But the particular implementations were better understood during early periods of history than in our present industrial society. For instance:

During the time of most of the Biblical writings, contacts of human beings with one another were face-to-face; rarely were there sizable group meetings. As a result, religious ethics have been influenced by the absence of large group contacts and all the attendant problems such as beset an industrial society.

The organization of these primitive communities was basically simple. Large, cooperative enterprises were unknown; the interdependence of management, capital, and labor on a massive scale was inconceivable.

Life moved at a slow pace, and varied but little. When change did come, it was likely to be by upheaval, not evolution.

The tremendous possibilities for an individual so characteristic of our world just were not available. The struggle for simple existence was a continuing and often futile effort; man's vision was limited both geographically and in the scope of the problems he faced. Rigid stratifications of all kinds determined the pattern of a man's life, and those of his children.

The state tended to be a hostile agent over which the individual had no control. Cooperative effort was rare; virtually no legal, accepted machinery existed for righting social and economic wrongs.

The possibility of a life hereafter assumed high importance because life on earth presented so few possibilities. Man's origins, still mysterious, were then shrouded in a complete darkness. Communication was undeveloped; mass education was impossible.

The impact of all these circumstances on the traditional applications of religion is incalculable. Take, for instance, the single problem of wealth. In the world of two thousand years ago, distribution of one man's riches to the poor had a real impact on his society. The giver was not entangled in complicated effects on the economy of the community because of a sudden withdrawal of capital from an enterprise. He did not have to worry about the response of the recipients; the damage to personal dignity and initiative was not important in a civilization where individual enterprise was neither a factor nor a possibility.

Or look at automation—and the complex problems involved in displacement of workers by new machines as set against the increased productivity of the whole society. Is automation "good" or "bad"? The answer depends on the time scale you are using and the group about whom you are talking.[2] The ancient teachers were faced with no such paradoxes—or, at least, not in that form.

Though attempts have been made throughout the centuries to reinterpret and realign religious teachings with the economic facts of the time, these efforts seem to have ground to a halt within the last century or so. Thus we are left heirs to the confusion which is inevitable when the words of two thousand years ago are sounded today.

"It's Never Been Done"

The church, its critics say, is departing from its historical role when it becomes involved in the problems of the day. It should stick to a man's soul and his salvation, which is its order of business and always has been. Again, we hear the recurring theme that "religion and business don't mix."

But the facts of the case are quite the opposite. Jesus himself demonstrated a lively concern with the issues of his time; as I have just pointed out, that interest of his has contributed to our confusion about the Scriptures today. Churchmen through the ages have turned their eyes to current issues. St. Thomas Aquinas held strong views on wealth and property; the Puritans of New England were not the first people to build a society around what they considered religious truths; the Popes have spoken out on public issues, and continue to do so now.

Of particular significance, John Calvin sought to apply religious teachings to economic realities in the sixteenth century—and in

[2] See Abram T. Collier, "Faith in a Creative Society," *Harvard Business Review*, May-June 1957, pp. 36-37.

so doing laid the basis for much of our current theology with his concept that it was man's duty to work diligently in whatever calling he might have chosen. Thus, acquiring wealth as a result of diligent work came to be looked on with favor and as the reward for Christian application to duty. The point of view that a life of poverty went hand in hand with piety gradually changed to the concept that a man should make the most of his God-given talents in his daily business.

There is no point in belaboring this matter; the record speaks for itself.

"Just a Front Group"

Christianity, it has been said, is primarily concerned with the justification of the capitalistic system. The accusation is valid to the extent that certain individuals have used Christianity to justify certain activities of their own. Marquis W. Childs and Douglass Cater, referring to the ecclesiastical outlook of the late Middle Ages, say:

It had come to the point where the church (at least the Protestant Church) was considered as scarcely more than a ceremonial ratification of the morality that prevailed.[3]

Likewise, Henry F. May writes that "in 1876 Protestantism presented a massive, almost unbroken front in its defense of the social status quo."[4] Of a later period, he makes the following statement:

Despite recurrent disclosure of corporate robbery, openhanded and enterprising captains of industry remained heroes to most Americans throughout the century. A large fraction of church opinion staunchly continued its unqualified defense of business and its leaders.[5]

Among the most severe critics of Christianity and its relation to the capitalistic system in this regard have been certain varieties of socialists. Their contention is that, because religious institutions receive a substantial portion of their financial support from prop-

[3] *Ethics in a Business Society* (New York, New American Library of World Literature, 1954), p. 136.
[4] *Protestant Churches and Industrial America* (New York, Harper & Brothers, 1949), p. 91.
[5] *Ibid.*, p. 130.

erty owners, "official church boards shape the policies of such organizations with an eye to continuing or increasing their receipt."[6] The socialists further claim that religious institutions along with newspapers, radio stations, and universities have great influence on public opinion; therefore, the policies of these agencies "are designed to protect and foster those institutions from which they draw their sustenance."[7]

John Ise has raised this same question:

> Since a few businessmen provide a considerable portion of the financial support of most churches, preachers often find it necessary to avoid discussion of problems of this earth, particularly labor problems; apparently our businessmen think it more important to prepare people for the next world than to make this one a more satisfactory place to live in.[8]

This interpretation of church-business relationships is held by many and denied by few. Any religious institution as well an any other institution with a major program must have financial support; and it is, likewise, logical to assume that necessary financial support will not be forthcoming if the institution is constantly or even periodically criticizing the source of the support.

The weakness of both the socialist contention and that of Ise is twofold:

(1) They are based on the assumption that property owners in our capitalistic system are a separate and distinct class apart from the remainder of the population.

(2) They assume there is a preferable system that could free the church from such control.

Property owners instead of being rare in the United States are a large portion of the entire population; and even those who do not own real estate or corporate stocks or bonds are not very different, for many of them have not acquired such items simply because of their personal choice to make other uses of their income and savings. Religious institutions in America receive their primary support from large numbers of small contributors; those receiving

[6] William N. Loucks and J. Weldon Hoot, *Comparative Economic Systems* (New York, Harper & Brothers, 1948), p. 309.

[7] *Ibid.*

[8] *Economics* (New York, Harper & Brothers, 1946), p. 550.

a substantial portion of their financial support from just a handful of very wealthy contributions are rare. Moreover, even in the case of those churches where most of the financial support comes from one or a few large sources, it is difficult to find definite indications that the basic policies followed differ much from the views of the smaller contributors.

But even if their criticisms are accurate, the socialists offer a still more unsatisfactory alternative. There is more likelihood of a close relationship between the expressions of religious institutions and their source of financial support when that support comes from the government. In such cases, coercive power is linked to financial control, and the effect is devastating. In countries where the church is state-supported, it is unlikely that its leaders will speak out against the government or against views held by political leaders for fear of retaliation.

Theoretically, it would be a good idea to have economic support of religious institutions completely independent of their teachings and policies, and we should surely try to divide the two as much as possible. But at the least we should seek to spread the burden of financial support over as wide an area as we can, calling on many different persons to contribute voluntarily.

Finally, I should point out that the fact that religious institutions exist and progress in a society in which the economic system is the capitalistic or free enterprise system does not mean that the religious institutions must have—or do have—the justification of the economic system as a major purpose.

"Guilt by Association"

A final accusation, related in some degree to the one which I have just discussed, is the so-called logic that declares, "Christianity and capitalism exist together; capitalism is bad; therefore Christianity is bad, too."

This "guilt by association" approach is typical of Karl Marx and his latter-day disciples. Marx, of course, was caustic about religion as such; it is "the opiate of the people," he solemnly declared. He complained that religion did not have a rational base. He was critical of the church for preaching about heaven in order to lessen the interest of people in improving worldly conditions. Marx contended that throughout the Middle Ages "the Church preached heaven, but strove to possess as much as possible of the earth."[9]

But the point is that Marx hated an economic system even more than he hated religion. His great antagonism to Christianity festered and grew because he associated it with an attempt to maintain an economic order which he wished to upset. In explaining the attitude of Marx toward Christianity, Professor Bober writes that Marx believed that "Christianity, when examined closely, is an earthly institution, and not the mother of elevated ethical ideals."[10] He states further that "as soon as it gained recognition by the state, the church eagerly joined the ranks of those engrossed in sordid affairs and enlisted itself as an agency of oppression."[11]

It is no surprise to anyone that Marx was not able to find in Christianity any help in bringing about the social order he advocated, or any support for the methods by which he urged that the new order be instituted. He wanted to destroy capitalism, and the methods he was willing to use meant that anything standing in the way had to be erased. Thus his real concern was with the economic system; his views on all else reflected his basic discontent with capitalism.

Unfortunately, Marx has no monopoly on accusations ostensibly hurled at religion but actually aimed elsewhere. How many people dislike *a* minister or *a* church or *a* doctrine and condemn the entire complex of tradition, aspiration, and belief! But our interest here is with the relationship between religion and an economic system.

Both have suffered in assaults on one another. We have witnessed attacks on the economic system which accuse it of being "unChristian"; but when we probe, we find that the real issue is something altogether different. The accuser does not care much whether or not the system is Christian; he is disturbed because it is not doing its job of production and distribution as he thinks it should be done. By the same token, Christianity has been on the receiving end of assaults as "irrational" or "the front for the status quo" when the attacker did not really care about Christianity one way

[9] M. M. Bober, *Karl Marx's Interpretation of History* (Cambridge, Harvard University Press, 1950), p. 152.

[10] *Ibid.*, p. 151.

[11] *Ibid.*

or the other; he was merely using this as one more weapon to club a social or an economic order.

What, then, is the relationship between an economic system—especially capitalism—and religion? Are their objectives opposed to one another? Is the promotion of economic well-being a "materialistic," ungodly pursuit?

No Conflict of Goals

There is not likely to be uniformity of agreement on the goals or objectives of our economic system. However, we can mark out several of its basic objectives which meet with general approval. One scholar has listed four objectives with which it is difficult to disagree:

1. A higher standard of living for all
2. Economic security and freedom
3. Production in accordance with consumer demands
4. An equitable distribution of income[12]

These interlocking objectives might be summarized as the greatest possible *economic* welfare, which includes both the highest standard of living achievable at the present time and even higher levels in the future. Each of these goals depends on and is related to the others, and one cannot be pursued to the exclusion of the rest.

Religion is much broader in scope than an economic—or political or social—structure, and religious goals are broader than economic. Without running the danger of unduly limiting them, the objectives of religion might be summarized as the greatest possible *human* welfare, as the fullest development of man, in all possible ways—physical, mental, *and* spiritual, economic *and* noneconomic—in accordance with the will of God. Must the goal of greatest possible economic welfare of society be in conflict with the noneconomic aspects of human welfare? If economic advance is achieved at the expense of other aspects of human well-being, then economic goals are of necessity in conflict with religion. If, however, a higher living standard does not require the sacrifice of

[12] George Leland Bach, *Economics, An Introductory Analysis* (New York, Prentice-Hall, Inc., 1957), p. 70.

broader human values in general, economic objectives are in harmony with religious goals. For, after all, greater economic welfare is a part of greater human welfare.

If religion and capitalism are rated according to importance, religion must unquestionably be number one since it, not some economic system, is the chief guide in the determination of the vital goals of life. Therefore, capitalism must conform to religious principles and objectives. If it does not, capitalism, not religion, must go. It would be unthinkable to discard a religion for not doing an effective job in justifying an economic system. The basic question should be: Does this particular economic approach of capitalism enable us more nearly to achieve basic religious goals than any other economic system?

A Better System

The socialist would, of course, answer *no*, in chorus with all those who advocate some other system. He would point out that the objectives listed above could be the goals of other types of economic systems—*with* some modifications, particularly freedom of choice as to how to engage one's productive resources, and production in response to consumer demand.

But the point is that these goals are much more likely to be realized under a free enterprise system. First, the capitalistic system affords the greatest stimulus to high and continuously increasing production. Therefore, it enables us to have a higher standard of living than would be attainable under any other system. It affords more freedom of choice in the use of productive resources and more freedom of choice on the part of consumers. No other system places as much emphasis on the freedom of the individual. In other words, capitalism is more harmonious with religion primarily because it works—because it does, in fact, advance human economic welfare.

It is true that capitalism has been widely criticized for its distribution of income. Undoubtedly certain other systems can provide for a more equitable distribution. After a formula for equity in distribution of income has been determined, several different systems might enable most of society to follow the formula at least as well—if not better—than free enterprise. But the great failure of other systems lies in the level of productivity they can achieve. Equitable distribution of less than a high and ever-increasing output of commodities and services inevitably leads to a low standard of living.

The mistake made by so many critics of our economic system is their failure to consider a combination of objectives, none of which should be ignored. Where these basic objectives have not been met, day-to-day operations have been to blame, not the system as such. It must be recognized, however, that these day-to-day failures are not unique to capitalism; they will be found anywhere. And free enterprise is more likely to correct such imperfections or breakdowns than is any other system yet devised.

Christianity and capitalism, then, are not in opposition to one another, although they are neither exactly parallel nor exact duplicates. Christianity is much broader in its approach to greater human welfare than is capitalism. While Christianity is concerned with the problem of the whole life of the individual and of better living for all mankind, capitalism is limited to the economic aspects of human society. The noneconomic aspects or phases of society are more extensive than are the economic. But since economic welfare is one important aspect of life, and a definite goal of the capitalistic system is greater economic welfare of all people, it is therefore not in opposition to Christianity and actually conforms to the basic religious goal of a better life for society as a whole.

Because the free enterprise system produces greater economic progress than would be possible under any other economic system known at the present, it is doing more to advance the broader goals of Christianity than could any other existing arrangement. Furthermore, there is no inherent reason why economic welfare under capitalism must be in any way at the expense of the general welfare; as a matter of fact, just the opposite is increasingly true. Nor is there reason to believe that the general welfare of society must or even will likely be reduced as a result of economic progress or greater economic welfare.

Capitalism and Democracy

In this discussion, I have been careful to differentiate between an economic system—capitalism—and a social and political system

—democracy. Obviously they are closely related to one another in theory, in history, and in fact. But nevertheless they are separate in that capitalism is essentially a type of *economic* organization while democracy is a *political* organization.

If, through some unhappy mischance, capitalism became interwoven with a political system of oppression and provided a continuous improvement in the standard of living at the expense of the basic individual freedoms as outlined in our Bill of Rights, it might still be in harmony with religion. But the total society of which it was a part would not be.

As a matter of fact, however, one of the great strengths of capitalism—and an attribute adding to its acceptability in religious terms—is that it can add to the preservation and expansion of human freedoms. It is philosophically and practically consistent with a free political system and contributes its influence to the fashioning of a free society which permits and encourages each individual to fulfill and develop his own talents and his own personality.

Conclusion

Whatever may be said of religions—or interpretations of spiritual teachings of the past—it is clear that the predominant religions in the United States today do not spell out the specific nature of an economic organization.

The American enterprise system developed long after Judaism and Christianity had many adherents, and religious goals cover much wider areas than just economic activity. Thus they can provide only a framework within which several forms of economic organizations might possibly be able to operate. The specific nature of an economic system, then, should not fall under the control of religion or of religious institutions such as churches and synagogues. By the same token, the system should not expect to be protected against all attacks and criticism; it should not look to the church for justification, though it certainly has a right to expect sympathy with its objectives. The fact that religious institutions seem to be in harmony with capitalism constitutes a compliment to the system rather than an obligation on the church to justify it.

Our experience in this country has been that the free enterprise capitalistic system most nearly complies with the religious principles and is at the same time the most productive. It is conceivable that one could describe a hypothetical system which might appear to operate more nearly in line with religious principles, but the weakness of the proposals made so far is that they do not work as well—do not turn out the goods. An economic system must work as well as conform to high ideals.

Incidentally, our critics frequently overlook the fact that many of the disadvantages they see arise from the degree of freedom inherent in our approach. Systems that do not provide economic and political freedom are unacceptable to us, and we are willing to put up with some shortcomings in order to protect that freedom. Further, it is imperative that any system which is in harmony with basic religious principles provide as much economic freedom as possible.

The Practicing Executive

The individual businessman is still left with the vitally important question: Can I be successful in business and at the same time work toward objectives which conform to my religious beliefs? It is difficult to see how we can expect full support of an economic system as a whole if we are unable to reconcile its day-to-day operation with our basic religious beliefs. Such support is seriously weakened by any widespread feeling that the activities of financial and industrial leaders are un-Christian. Consequently, the fact that we are following an economic system which conforms to the basic concepts of Christianity is not enough; we have to raise the question of whether the work of each businessman follows the same basic concepts.

It is, of course, perfectly possible for individual businessmen to ignore religious teachings in their quest for personal economic gain. It is, likewise, conceivable for this to be done even on a national basis. Though this may not be the fault of the system any more than it is Christianity's fault that at various periods of history certain individuals and groups have acted in an un-Christian way in the name of Christianity, it still poses a tough question: Is Christianity workable in the business world, or must we be content with saying that the objectives and general principles of free enterprise are in harmony with religion?

I believe that an executive can conduct his business in harmony with religious principles without subjecting it to undue risks. The religious teachings of Judaism and Christianity do not either of them provide specific answers to every business or economic problem any more than they offer clear-cut solutions to the many noneconomic problems. However, both religions provide a framework or set of principles and values in which successful businessmen may operate. Given a sense of confidence in the harmonious relationship between religion and our capitalistic system, each businessman can proceed to work out his own code and operating philosophy for his own situation.

11.

Business and the Good Society

By Raphael Demos*

Political democracy, Protestantism, capitalism, science and the new learning are, in important ways, aspects of one and the same historic trend. They all herald the rise of individualism and the decay of authority which marked the passing of the Middle Ages. Enterprise—both in thought and action—gradually became the property of individuals, instead of a few central groups. Just as the Protestant insisted on reading the Bible for himself, so did the scientist insist on reading the book of nature for himself. Thus, with the emergence of the new world:

In politics, a host of conflicting nations flourished, and within the nations a host of parties.

In religion, the Protestant sects multiplied indefinitely.

In the economic field, the competition of the various business units developed.

In learning, the towering medieval synthesis crashed into the various unrelated specialties of science. The seamless garment of knowledge and society was torn to pieces.

In a word—and in a sense—chaos replaced cosmos. Yet the chaos with its freedom became creative, as in the mythical cosmogonies. Individualism is the face of Helen that launched the thousand ships of Western modern civilization.

* Mr. Demos is Alford professor of natural religion, moral philosophy, and civil polity at Harvard University.

181

INDIVIDUALISM AND CHANGE

Whereas authoritarianism is attachment to a single pattern of to a fixed dogma, individualism is experimental, tentative, an changeful. For instance, science is innovation—the perpetual r vision of old theories and the advance to novelty. Likewise th entrepreneurial activity of the capitalist results in something mo than an increased production of existing types of goods; it create novel forms of goods and novel patterns of enterprise. Again, science is experimental, testing theories by the observed facts, so democracy experimental, testing one party against another b appeal to the voting public.

Open Systems

Karl Popper has introduced into our thinking the highly valu able concept of the *open society* in his brilliant work with tha title.[1] A closed society, having shut its doors to any new pattern is hostile to change, while an open society is fluid because it hospitable to alternative forms of life. Likewise a closed mind dogmatic, being content with what it regards as the absolute trutl while an open mind welcomes dissent and controversy. Such dive sity of doctrines is like competition in business, while intellectu authoritarianism is monopolistic.

Democracy is an open political system. There is always the po sibility that the minority will become a majority and thus revers the government. The citizen of a monolithic government has n alternatives, but in a democracy the voter has a variety of parti and issues to choose from. Correspondingly, free enterprise is a open economy; the consumer may pick from one of several bran and do his shopping in any store. A totalitarian economy provid only one brand at one store, so to speak, for the public to buy else do without.

Checks and Balances

The division of powers, the system of checks and balances, the expression in the field of government of the doctrine tha monopoly is dangerous everywhere. Human beings are finite, su ject to the temptations of pride and power, and relatively ignoran

[1] *Open Society and Its Enemies* (Princeton, Princeton University Press, 195

They need each other both as a check and as compensation for their own insufficiency:

In the realm of intellectual thought, I need your criticism and you need mine.

In government, democracy provides a similar flow of criticism from every direction. No ruler, not even the wisest, knows enough; no ruler, not even the best, is immune to the temptations of total power. In a government by the many, it becomes possible for the limited personal perspective of a particular individual to be supplemented by the equally finite viewpoint of the others.

In the economic sphere, the same principle means that no business should be so powerful that it can ignore the checks of other economic units, or of other social institutions, or of society as a whole. In its own way, competition in business corresponds to mutual criticism in the field of learning.

Same Kind of Freedom

Freedom of thought and freedom of business enterprise are not so different, after all. In both, the individual is exposed to a diversity of alternatives. In both, there is the friction of competition and the spark of progress that it generates. Both declare for a free market: the one in ideas, the other in goods. Yet an undeclared war rages between the businessman and the academician, with each side demanding a severe curtailment, if not an abolition, of the freedoms of the other:

The businessman, while insisting on immunity from control for himself, argues for a restriction of academic freedom. Conversely, the intellectual is apt to clamor for a political control of business while energetically upholding freedom of thought.

The businessman, and indeed the ordinary citizen, will point out that freedom of speech and thought may lead to dangerous and erroneous views. The professor insists that unfettered business enterprise leads often to ruthlessness and social injustice.

The businessman defends the freedom of his enterprise by arguing that such evils are the minor price we must pay for that release of activity which ensures the greatest possible productivity. The academician likewise argues that occasional errors—his errors—are the minor cost we must incur for that free market of ideas which ensures the maximum achievement of truth.

The time has come for a truce in this cold war. It is well to remind the businessman that academic freedom is almost the last remaining stronghold of free enterprise; it is well to remind the academician that, other things being equal, freedom in material production is better than its absence. I do not mean to deny the necessity of regulation and control, here and there, of business enterprise. Of this, indeed, I will have something to say later. Nevertheless, control from within and self-discipline, when they can be had, are preferable to control from without.

It is said, often truly, that the businessman who talks of free enterprise is actually aiming at a monopoly. But it is also true that the thinker who insists on the right of dissent, as long as he himself is in a minority, tends to become authoritarian and intolerant of opposing views when his own become generally accepted. An idea which prevails tends to harden into a dogma; and a business enterprise which succeeds tends to become dominating. It is human nature to wish freedom for no one but oneself. Kipling once wrote a story with the title "The Man Who Would Be King." Now, that man is everyman.

As with many wars, a good deal of informal traffic goes on between the hostile parties. The businessman confides his sons and daughters to the wooly-minded professor for their education; and the latter receives money for scholarships and college buildings from the businessman. Fundamentally, the hostilities arise from unconscious and irrational attitudes; they express the instinctive distrust that men of action and men of thought feel for each other. These attitudes are also an oblique manifestation of a feeling of inferiority on the part of each group toward the other. Let us understand them for what they are and work to obliterate them.

The important thing to remember is that it is the same kind of freedom which marks both liberal thought and dynamic capitalism.

OUR DYNAMIC ECONOMY

The fact that capitalism has been dynamic in this country, unlike some others, is due to the beneficent influence of the American ethos. We have favored social mobility and believed in equal opportunity for all. Especially because of such opportunity in education, our society has become as fluid as it is. We have avoided a rigid class structure, thus making it almost impossible for revolutionary parties to succeed. On the whole, labor has accepted our political system, while in Europe revolutions have been proclaimed by and for the proletariat. In this country, the laborer has not thought of himself as a proletarian; he has not felt himself sentenced by fate to a low status and a low living standard.

Some factors, of course, are peculiarly responsible for dynamism in our economy, as opposed to those which supply the vigor to our society as a whole. For example, business has operated on the implicit premise that human wants are infinite and that there is no ceiling to the expansion of our economy. Let us analyze this concept of material wants.

Man's Expanding Needs

It is sometimes assumed that human beings have a fixed number of material needs clamoring for satisfaction. Economic activity is taken as a response to these needs; when their satisfaction is accomplished, our economy is supposed to level out. Poverty, in this view, reflects the fact that a human being is deprived of these necessary satisfactions, while wealth means the opposite.

While admitting that there is a minimum of fixed basic material desires, I will argue that thereafter there is no limit to what we may want, and that consequently neither poverty nor wealth has an absolute meaning. You are not rich if you own x number of goods, and poor if you fall short of that number. You are rich if you are *content* with what you own, and poor if you are dissatisfied —presuming that you have gone beyond the minimum.

What is it, then, that man needs? He needs what he wants, and he wants what he can think about. My parents did not need radios; they had not heard of them. But I need a radio at home; I get one and am satisfied. Or am I? Perhaps I need another to keep upstairs, and the children need their own since they listen to programs for which I do not care. How many homes does a man need? I own one; some people own none; J. P. Morgan, I believe, owned a dozen. Was he, then, extravagant? Yet he found a use for them all.

People agitate to get more goods for themselves, not only because they suffer but often because they have become more enlightened.

So, beyond a certain minimum, poverty and riches are relative to a conventional standard of living. And the latter is like an elevator continually rising; as soon as the majority have reached the level which the few have enjoyed, then the standard is lifted to a higher floor. The poor man of today is, in some ways, richer than the Pharaohs of old, for he lives in cities with better roads and sanitation than the Pharaohs dreamt of. No sooner do we cease being poor than we become poor once more, because the scale of living has been upped.

Needs emerge as the human mind envisages new possibilities of material satisfaction. The stimulus for change comes from the human imagination, which is a property not of artists only but of all active humans. In this context, the function of advertising becomes clearer. The advertiser creates new wants and needs by opening up new vistas to the human imagination. He creates the wants, while the producer creates the goods to satisfy them. This is not to cast a blanket approval on frequent current practices—the raucousness, the poor taste, the high-pressure techniques. It is only to assert that in an expanding economy advertising plays a necessary and valid role.

Finally, to the extent that material production has been geared to an indefinitely expanding number of wants, economic activity has tended to become an end in itself, an immediate manifestation of the creative energies of man. Of course, for the businessman production has been governed by profit; but, from the point of view of society as a whole, the increase in the number and quality of goods has operated as an expression of the desire for life and life more abundant.

Not for Export

As already noted, our type of capitalism is partly determined by our way of life, which favors mobility. Of course, this pattern of mobility is partly a reflection of environmental forces; for the American continent has great and greatly diversified natural resources. Yet it is also true that mobility is a way of life which we prefer and believe in to a special degree.

The fact that our American system of free enterprise is bound up with the American ethos of equal opportunity for all should make us wary of proposing it for our European friends. In Europe, capitalism has been part of a different social outlook. It has been associated with a rigid social stratification, stemming from feudalism. Thus, in Europe, both labor and the middle classes equate capitalism with privilege and power on the one hand, and with oppression and poverty on the other. Indeed, the very word *capitalism* has a different meaning on the far side of the Atlantic.

It may be that, there, the removal of inequality and class privilege has priority over more strictly economic problems. It is from this perspective that the welfare state in England should be viewed. Superficially, the welfare state looks like socialism; essentially it is the battle against class divisions and other remnants of feudalism. If this interpretation be correct, the welfare state may be considered only as an intermediate step; so that once its real aims are achieved, it will (let us hope) give place to a system in which productivity and private enterprise emerge as paramount.

Paying the Piper

At the same time, we should not forget that this particular way of life which we have chosen exacts payments for the benefits it bestows. You never get something for nothing, in business or in life! Thus, it is doubtful that our system makes for peace of mind. Wide horizons stimulate the imagination; they also exhaust the nervous system. Mobility creates fearful hazards with inevitable attendant anxieties; already we hear demands for security on behalf of labor and business as well.

In order to realize the full implications of our pattern, let us contrast it with that of Epicurus, the Greek philosopher who lived in the fourth and third centuries B.C.:

Epicurus asserted that tranquillity is the greatest of human goods; and in order to obtain it, he confined his life within the privacy of a garden. The world of affairs is like a jungle full of lurking dangers, and it must be avoided. Man, said Epicurus, must shun politics and all involvements in the larger context of life and society. He must not even have family ties, with their risks and obligations. He must have only friendships, for friends can be changed at will. Furthermore, they form a sort of bodyguard, protecting a man from the slings and arrows of a hostile world.

Tranquillity meant for Epicurus a removal from the life of action. He condemned what he called the kinetic (or active) desires which lead men to alter circumstances; he preferred the static desires which induce man to accept and adjust himself to existing situations. He gave high praise to the condition of a static equilibrium. To secure this state, Epicurus was willing to simplify his wants to the point of austerity.

Epicurus was the first thinker of the Western world to proclaim freedom from fear as the greatest good. And he was willing to pay the price for his ideal: he renounced ambition and the dynamic impetus of life itself. Compare his pattern with ours:

We favor the kinetic desires. We are restlessly active, paying the price in worry and stomach ulcers.

We like publicity, and go out of our way to create it. (Epicurus' motto was: "Live unnoticed.")

We value change for its own sake; we build and then we unbuild.

We insist on productive work, and cherish ambition.

We believe less in gardens than in cities. Instead of quiet, we have noise and plenty of it.

We are joiners; and when organizations are lacking, we bring them about.

We do not believe in the simple life; we believe in the complex life. Not austerity but comfort is our ideal.

We like to take risks, and peace of mind is a fast-fading vista.

But this is the choice we have made; and I hope we shall stick to it, never giving up mobility in our search for security.

My aim in the above account has been to show that capitalist economy basically is no isolated phenomenon, not a biological sport in our culture, but part of an all-inclusive system of concepts and values involving religion, politics, education, and science. In short, capitalist economy is an aspect of a complex and organic unity. The common denominator in all these areas has been the stress on freedom, fluidity, spontaneous activity. Indeed, as soon as man becomes conscious of himself as a rational being, he overcomes the fatalistic attitude toward life and becomes dynamic, modifying his status, his environment, instead of being resigned to it. This is because his reason, or rather his imagination, presents him with ever new possibilities.

Need to Control Vitality

I have suggested that we are paying, and will continue to pay, for our choice of a way of life, just as Epicurus paid for his. But we have now reached the point where we are actively concerned with cutting the costs. We are confronting problems, occasioned by the release of independent power, in all areas:

Democracy is constantly threatened by private pressures, by regional and other vested interests. The evils of unchecked nationalism are too obvious to mention.

Protestantism is in a state of near anarchy and seems to be disintegrating into a shower of unconnected and even conflicting sects.

Even science, once heralded by secular reformers as the answer to all the questions posed by the human predicament, is now viewed with some suspicion, and its practitioners are sometimes felt to be Frankensteins.

Problems of Quick Growth

Business made tremendous strides once it became allied with science. As science has produced technological and industrial innovations, so has business expanded and proliferated. We have experienced an accelerated production of an increasing variety of material goods, with an attendant rise of the standard of living for everybody.

But sudden and quick changes bring severe dislocations in their train. Consider, for instance, the social effects of the invention of the automobile—its effects on custom, its importance in opening up new opportunities and new dangers for the moral life and the life of the mind. Note, further, that the social changes brought about by scientific and industrial advance are entirely unplanned and unforeseen; they are not unlike natural catastrophes or what the lawyers call "acts of God."

The natural scientist is, of course, incapable of coping by his own methods with the social dislocations for which he, along with the businessman, is responsible. When James Watt contrived the condensing steam engine, his purpose was simply to improve the pumping of water in the mines; he did not envisage his invention as having anything to do with railways. But, supposing he had thus envisaged it, was it possible for him at that time to anticipate the enormous impact of the railway system, not only on transportation but on the general life of people? And even had he been able to anticipate these results, did he as an engineer have the method (not to say the power) to cope with them?

Goods and Happiness

We are faced, then, with the complex and painful task of assimilating into our social ways the many and various products which are coming off our assembly lines. It is not enough to put the food into your mouth; you have to chew and digest it. We have naïvely been assuming that it was sufficient to make the goods available for human beings and human satisfaction would follow automatically. But an increase of goods does not necessarily mean an increase of human satisfaction. Too many goods made available too quickly may produce only social indigestion.

We speak of prosperity as though it were an economic concept—an abundance of goods, of employment, of buying and selling. Prosperity is primarily a psychological and social concept; prosperity means human welfare—the good life in society. It is hardly an exaggeration to say that unless the scientist-cum-businessman is also a citizen, society may perish. Above all, he must constantly remember that the making of goods is incidental and subordinate to the making of men.

Thus large-scale industry—the child born from the marriage of business and science—has created grave problems by its abrupt and quick growth. Though aiming at increased comfort, in many ways we have more discomfort than before. Often the pace of work is enervating; we are in too much of a hurry. Large cities provide new aids for living; and yet, in a curious fashion, they have really diminished the amenities. Spaciousness is vanishing. We live in cramped and microscopic quarters. Buildings are getting bigger, but living space is getting smaller. Our streets are crowded, smoky, and excessively noisy.

In mass production, pride of skill is reduced to a minimum, for what is there to enjoy when the product is only a fragment? Compare this with the medieval craftsman who made the complete product and so was able to use both skill and art in adjusting piece to piece into a harmonious whole. Furthermore, city life and concentration on manufactured goods have tended to cut modern man off from his own sources in primitive nature. Yet an intuitive feeling of harmony with nature is essential to the renewal of our energies. We talk of freedom, but how far are we free in our work, how far does the individual count—whether executive or worker—in our vast business enterprises? The worker himself is always under orders, and it is hard to see how a person who is a cog in a machine at his work can operate as a free human being in his leisure.

Loneliness and Leisure

In our modern world, society is vanishing from our lives—I mean society as a *person-to-person* relationship. We get lost in the crowd. Note how we insist on calling one another by first names even when we hardly know each other. In the small group, we are known for ourselves and can be judged at our true worth. But in the great society, we are known to others, if at all, by publicity only; and publicity can be created artificially and may deceive.

While physically closer to one another in the cities (I mean the fact that my apartment may adjoin yours), we are more estranged than ever before. The street of the small town was also a neighborhood. Aristotle prescribed that the size of a city should be so limited as to enable the town crier's voice to be heard by every citizen at the same time. Now that we have radio broadcasting, Aristotle's requirement seems absurdly out of date. Yet he had a point. My sense of security depends on what my fellows think of me; I need to belong to a group small enough so that I may be personally known by all its members.

And what about leisure? One of the strongest articles of faith for social reformers has been the need of leisure for everyone, especially the workingman. Today it seems that the ideal is near attainment; many of us have a five-day week. Yet it is doubtful that people have true leisure. Just to have empty time on your hands is like holding an empty cup; you must find something to pour into it. Where leisure is concerned, it must be your own liquid substance. Use of leisure is a skill to be learned; otherwise there is simply a vacuum, not filled either by the reading of the

Sunday papers, the sponging-up of a TV show, or the passive listening to mechanically transmitted music, mostly of the flimsiest quality.

Leisure is not the mere absence of work. It is activity, but one to which you are not driven. It is an activity which is not a duty. More than freedom, leisure means the recovery of one's natural spontaneous self and its reactivation. Work is the macadam road, and leisure is the green country, but sometimes leaving the road means falling into the ditch. The actual situation creates a vicious circle; because the work is likely to be meaningless and onerous, people seek to fill up their free time with neurotic excitement, which is anything but leisurely. Good leisure can come only from good work.

In short, we have discovered that vitality is apt to go wild unless controlled. We must now humanize and civilize our society by regulating it with a concept of the general good of man. We must look beyond our own immediate interests to the rights and needs of others, beyond economic values to human values.

The Dilemma of Business

Does this mean, particularly, that we must control the vitality of business?

Certainly, some thoughtful people would dispute the proposition that free enterprise and a good society are two sides of the same coin. They feel that business is inherently evil—albeit a necessary evil—and not part of a good society. In this view, the abuses and excesses in business are not simply exceptions but rather the symptoms of an incurable malady:

Business is essentially materialistic, an expression of the lower human impulses, such as greed.

Business creates an acquisitive society, hostile to spiritual ideals, ruled by Mammon. For instance, the Bible declares that the love of money is the root of all evil, asserting in picturesque language that it is harder for a rich man to enter the kingdom of heaven than for a camel to go through the eye of a needle. The implication seems to be that a man cannot be both a Christian and a successful businessman.

Economic activity involves planning, reckoning profit against loss. But "consider the lilies of the field how they grow; they toil not, neither do they spin: And yet I say unto you, that even Solomon in all his glory was not arrayed like one of these."

We are urged to lay up our treasures in heaven. Business piles its treasures on the earth; its values are secular.

These criticisms reduce basically to two: (a) that business deals with material goods, hostile to spiritual values; (b) that the motivation of the businessman is self-interest—the making of money.

Material or Spiritual

Of course business deals with material goods. But surely business is the response to *all* satisfactions, not material ones alone. A publisher selling books of poetry or an art dealer selling paintings is surely meeting spiritual needs. Economic activity is the exchange and flow through the body politic of all goods, whether physical or cultural. Everything has a price and can be bought. The catch is that it cannot be bought unless it exists; that is, unless it has been produced. On the other hand, cultural goods cannot be produced by business; only the artist can create the painting; only the scientist can yield the scientific discovery. In this sense, then, it is a fact that business is confined to the area of material goods.

Even so, there is no reason for believing that secular values are hostile to spiritual values. The earth can provide a ladder to heaven, though many people trip and fall in the process of climbing. My car enables me to get to the place where I can hear a lecture which improves my mind. Our various domestic appliances make for health, which is good for the soul; also for cleanliness, which is next to godliness. We hear much about the depersonalizing impact of machinery; yet machinery, by diminishing arduous physical labor, makes man less of a beast of burden.

Industrial civilization, to the extent that it eliminates squalor, contributes to the spiritual dignity of man. Man cannot live by bread alone; nor can he live without it. To condemn material things because they are material is to exhibit a snobbishness of the spirit which is as bad as social snobbishness.

Mixed Motives

The professions are not supposed to be governed by such self-seeking motives as is business:

Medicine has always included charity and free service, not merely profit. Medicine is governed by the Hippocratic oath. A great surgeon is one who has performed notable surgical cures, no matter how he may have fared financially.

A teacher must of course make a living; but, beyond that, he is actuated by a direct concern for the intellectual welfare of his students.

Likewise, a scientist will spend many extra hours in the laboratory, analyzing his specimens, measuring his chemical substances, not because this will increase his income but from the restless desire for truth, haunting and persecuting him like a fury.

So is a civil servant or a military officer motivated by love of country. And law is for justice.

But business is . . . business.

Can the assumptions about motivations, underlying such a contrast between business and the professions, be accepted? Is it true that the professional man is simply governed by ideal desires, while the businessman's aim is simply to make money? Surely, the sheep and the goats are not distinguished among human beings just by their occupations! If they were, St. Peter would have a very easy time of it at the Eternal Gates.

There are saints and sinners in every occupational group. If the businessman is after profits, is not the politician after votes? It is always difficult to look into the human heart and discern motives —all the more difficult because self-interest has a way of disguising itself in elegant clothing. After all, love of money is not the only form which self-interest can take. There is also love of power, love of distinction, love of glory:

The military officer does not get rich on his pay, but surely he likes his rank, his decorations, and his glory.

Is the teacher wholly altruistic? Perhaps he experiences the pleasure of exerting power over younger minds.

The scientist, devoted as he is to the truth, also wants to make a great name for himself.

Conversely, we may question whether the businessman works just for money. The fact is that, in normal cases, a young man goes into business because he likes it, just as some other young man goes into philosophy because he likes *that*. After he goes in, the businessman does indeed look for profits. But it is too simple to equate profit with personal gain; profit includes salary for services rendered, and reserves for depreciation and new investment. And when the gain is personal, there is the fact that a great deal of it, in this country, has been contributed by the businessman to the support of educational, religious, and charitable institutions. We may call it conscience money or a symptom of delayed idealistic response.

But, to repeat, it is hard to disentangle motives. Does a business-man seek money for its own sake or also because money is the socially recognized criterion for accomplishment? In other words, is not business activity also a manifestation of the impulse to build, to establish a going and growing concern—an impulse analogous to that of the creative artist? The answer is that it is not this or that impulse alone, but actually a mixture of all of them. The crucial question then arises: Which is the preponderant motive?

On the whole, I believe that in the traditional professions the ideal of the social good has been and will remain more in control of self-interest than in business. This is not to say that the business-man, *as a human being,* differs from other men as regards moral ends. It is rather that he tends to live a divided life, stressing self-interest inside his business while expressing his social impulses out-side it. (Of course, I am exaggerating. There is no career where the rules of honesty and of the honoring of contracts are as stringently respected as in business. Such honesty is practically intrinsic to the structure of business.)

But this does not mean that business is inherently *evil,* that its freedom is not equivalent to, or as important as, political and intellectual freedom. It simply means that some of its dynamics are different. It also means that external regulation of its freedom is more likely and more necessary than control of freedom in other areas.

SOCIAL RESPONSIBILITY

The crucial question, then, is: Given the particular circumstances and nature of business, how can we cut the costs of freedom and control the excesses of vitality? Can business itself contribute to the attempt we are making to preserve the strengths and eliminate the strains of our way of life, or is business unable to make these adjustments and still preserve its vigor and its essential character?

External and Internal Pressures

Certainly, there is no point in going as far as socialism, just because business cannot control itself perfectly. Socialism is based on the premise that private enterprise and social outlook are mutually incompatible, and that only government—the organized force of the community—can look to the public good. But government bureaucracy is not necessarily socially minded. Pride of power and love of gain can overtake government officials no less than the rest of us. Furthermore, imagination, inventiveness, and drive are primarily—though not exclusively—the property of private individuals.

Besides, the power of business no longer is unlimited. It is now confronted by the power of government, on the one hand, and that of organized labor, on the other. The times are past when business could issue orders, "take it or leave it"; now business must negotiate with other powers and make compromises. I am not suggesting that labor and government are in themselves *moral* powers. What we have here is the old democratic device of checks and balances; and the good, such as it is, comes from the ability of each power to restrict the others. In short, we have competition again, though on another plane. And in the background lurks the informal, wavering conscience of the community, voiced in the press, from the pulpit, and by other manifold groups.

More important, we know from experience that in the professions it *is* possible for self-interest to be subordinated to the public good. Why should not the same be true in business? After all, we are all more or less alike. The businessman and the judge may be brothers bred and brought up by the same parents in the same environment.

The trustees of a college, for example, act up to their name and govern it as stewards of a public trust although it may be privately owned and managed. May not business be infused with a like sense of stewardship?

Or take law in its relation to justice. When the law has seemed to operate unjustly upon individuals, the judges have appealed to equity or have invoked the clause of "due process." This concept is almost wholly indefinite, but its very indefiniteness has enabled the judges to use it as a weapon in favor of justice and conscience. Cannot business, too, have its own clause of due process?

Unrealistic Expectation

Gradually, internal, built-in checks are becoming part of business, and there is a growing sense of mutuality and loyalty within a business unit. Nevertheless, I think it would be unrealistic to expect business to be conducted exactly like a profession—and for two good reasons:

(1) The professions have explicitly formulated standards by which their own members may be tested. A lawyer has to pass his state bar examinations, and a would-be doctor must pass his appropriate tests. There are no such entrance requirements for a businessman, and I doubt that any could be devised, or even that they should be. The element of "art" or hunch in business, the element of luck, and even the element of requisite freedom will always be there to distinguish business from the professions.

(2) In contrast to material goods, spiritual goods are infinite. The fact that I have obtained knowledge does not make it any harder for you to obtain it also. In fact, it makes it easier. The fact that one person enjoys a given piece of music does not prevent some other person from enjoying it. In other words, cultural goods are not used up by being enjoyed but can be shared without being exhausted.

But, if I own this dollar bill, you cannot own it; if you own this piece of land or this car, I do not have it. In this sense economic goods are finite; *economy* and *scarcity* are equivalent words. There is only so much or so little to go around. While spiritual goods unite us, material goods will divide us and tend to create a condition of war among human beings.

Any individual in his everyday living is occupied with the endless conflict between appetite and reason, vitality and morality. To achieve the good life, he must be helped by external sanctions. The point is that this applies more to the businessman as a businessman than to the professional as a professional. That is why we cannot wholly rely on the developing conscience of the businessman, but must also look to power checks from without (such as government and other organized groups like labor) and to the informal influence of public opinion.

Guiding Principles

What, then, are the specific ways in which business will show its increasing sense of social responsibility? I do not think I can give the answer. Indeed, it is doubtful that anyone can lay down in advance specific programs for business. Such matters will have to be worked out empirically in answer to particular challenges as they arise. But one may suggest some general formulas as guiding principles for action:

(1) Laws may be necessary; but, other things being equal, freedom is better than law. When a good thing is done by compulsion, its goodness is diminished. When it is done willingly, its goodness is enhanced. Preserve the freedom of the producer as much as is feasible while at the same time protecting the public. More and more, we should count on education to do the job of law. For example, if a worthless (but harmless) patent medicine goes on the market priced way above cost, should we legislate the product out? I do not think it is the task of government to save the public from its own follies. Rather let us improve the judgment of the public by better schooling.

(2) The basic consideration of profits in business must be supplemented by the factor of the social good. To take an example: Here is a plant which will have to be relocated because profits are larger elsewhere. What will such a change mean to the employees and also to the region itself? Some balance must be struck between profits and social responsibility.

(3) The general assumption has heretofore been that business discharges its social function *indirectly,* by raising the general standards of living. This is not enough; business also has a direct responsibility for the material welfare of the community, and the only question is whether the businessman must discharge this responsibility as a private individual —after hours, so to speak—or in his capacity as a businessman.

(4) Beyond material welfare, the businessman must contribute to the cultural and spiritual welfare of the community and the nation. Increasingly, the American businessman has been playing the role which, in older times, the aristocracy played in Europe. In this country, he has been and is the patron of culture, supporting education, musical organizations, and the fine arts. But here a word of caution may be in order: being a patron must not be confused with a patronizing attitude. There is already a prevailing fear of business power.

Business, so jealous of its own independence, must equally respect the independence and integrity of the cultural life which it supports. We know that in the early days of the century the railways tended to control state legislatures. But control of government by business is as much to be condemned as control of business by government. Educational institutions have their own methods and standards, developed slowly through the centuries; and only as education is wholly self-governing can it fulfill its task. In short, the businessman as patron must resist any temptation to dominate the cultural enterprises which he so generously supports.

(5) Earlier I commented on the fact that people have very little freedom in their work. While this is true of labor primarily, it is also true of employees in general, and even of executives at the junior levels. Perhaps as many as four out of five of us are employees working for someone else. Now, work is such a dominating part of our lives that no matter how well we may live outside it, we cannot be living a good life unless we live that life in our work as well. Freedom and the consciousness of being significant and participating members of an enterprise are essential factors in the happiness of everyone. How can these be secured for the worker?

I should make it clear that I do not believe in self-government in business; management must be in charge. This means that business is authoritarian; and indeed the principle of authority has a rational basis in business. It is the expert who must make the decisions; authority derives from knowledge. Thus, in the professions, no one would claim that the doctor should consult his secretary about a diagnosis.

But this seems to leave us with a contradiction: authoritarianism is necessary in business, and authoritarianism is bad. While I have no solution, it is important for us to understand that the present situation is not satisfactory in any final sense. At least the businessman should be keenly aware of the existence of this problem, realizing that it may often account for discontent among labor even when the economic factors are satisfactory.

The Religious Impulse

I have one further suggestion, and I advance it tentatively for the businessman to ponder. After all, he is the one who should know whether ideals can be practical in industry, whether an enterprise can be run on something more than self-interest.

Paradoxically enough, the suggestion comes from a phenomenon that has been observed in Communism. No doubt Communist enterprise is less efficient than ours on a per-unit production basis, and we all abhor the bases of the Communist program. But some of the Communist accomplishments are almost beyond understanding. Is there a clue here to some kind of motivation that we could apply in the setting of our own precious beliefs and values?

In this connection, let me quote from Donald K. David, former dean of the Harvard Business School:

> In that portion of the world dominated by the most materialistic creed in history—the area behind the iron curtain—the ideology in terms of complete devotion to a cause is essentially like a religion. In the Western World, whose philosophy is spiritual in origin and whose freedom is a magnificent cause, for all men the outlook of life, society, and progress is mostly expressed in quantitative terms. We are said to think in terms of wealth, of material things.[2]

What a paradox, indeed, and how shall we explain it? How can we account for the fact that Communism has exercised such an appeal on people, especially the young? There is, of course, no simple answer. For many it has meant opportunity for power, for others the hope of overcoming their poverty. But this does not explain why it has had the appeal of religion.

The power of Communism in certain areas has come from the fact that, instead of *offering* people everything, Communism has asked them to *give* everything—to give and give utterly. We in this country have tended to take a "realistic" view, assuming that the only way to get something out of a person is by showing how much there is in it for him. Yet in all of us there is the urgent need to dedicate ourselves to a cause beyond self. The Communists have recognized this need and exploited it for their own ends. A man will rather surrender himself to a *false* god than to no god at all, and this is the sense in which Communism has appeared in the guise of a religion to many.

The Communists have stolen their weapons from our own Christian armory, where they have been lying neglected and rusting. In fighting Communism, it is important to recover our weapons and use them. We must appeal once more to the self-transcending impulses in human nature.

[2] Edward C. Bursk, Editor, *Getting Things Done in Business* (Cambridge, Harvard University Press, 1953), p. 48.

We have been talking of religion. Now, the religious impulse exists in all of us, and its essence lies in the urge to rise above private gain and satisfaction and to surrender oneself to an ideal. Let us not be so foolishly "practical" as to ignore its existence. It is a significant comment on our civilization that spontaneously we all regard Albert Schweitzer, who chose a life of service over the prospects of a highly successful career in any one of several fields, as different from ordinary men; but perhaps it is even more significant that our civilization does produce such a person from time to time.

Moreover, it *is* possible to gain the assent of youth to a reasonable proposal by saying to them: "There is nothing of gain for you in this; there is every opportunity for you to give." During the war, many citizens, including businessmen, gave freely of time, energy, and money (not to speak of life) for their country. However, I am not saying that human beings are saints; self-interest is also there with its own strains and pulls. After all, the war was a supreme crisis; in peacetime, the self-transcending desires are liable to become torpid, weaker than self-interest. (Perhaps this fact partly explains why the Communists have to create a perpetual war crisis in order to induce their public to make the sacrifices demanded of them.)

All I am saying is that maybe somehow, sometime, businessmen can get more of this feeling into themselves and their enterprises. The same approach might help politicians and professionals too, but I am thinking of it here as a way out of the particular dilemma of businessmen.[3]

Note that I have been making suggestions, not proposing definite solutions. After all, it would be improper for an outsider to preach to businessmen. Rather it is the duty of businessmen themselves to find the solutions, viewing the problems as challenges clamoring to be met. The task of thinking out solutions for these long-run issues is one primarily for the man who knows business from the inside. Likewise, it is the responsibility of our business schools, with all the time and information that they have at their disposal, to

[3] For one businessman's ideas on this point, see O. A. Ohmann, " 'Skyhooks' (With Special Implications for Monday Through Friday)," *Harvard Business Review*, May-June 1955, p. 33; also p. 70 of this volume.—*Editor.*

analyze and provide insights into these problems. It is not enough
for a business school to turn out young men capable of operating
in the existing structure of business; it is also its function—and
perhaps its greater function—to think out new and improved
patterns of business operations.

CONCLUSION

How far is it possible for business to approach the pattern of
the professions, or how far may a businessman practice within his
business the social feelings which he expresses outside it? After all,
business has as much of a social purpose as any profession. For instance, the function of medicine is to provide health to society;
analogously, that of business is to procure goods and services for
society.

Of course, business cannot be run as a charity, if only because
charity itself depends on the profits of business. Business must be
technically efficient and financially solvent. Yet this is not inconsistent with the proposition that business must recognize the human
rights of employees and the public, no less than of stockholders
and management. For business involves a direct relation not only
to things but to human beings as well. The things are made by
human beings, namely by labor; and they are made for human
beings, that is to say, the consumers. A civilized moral ideal requires that human beings be treated as ends, not as commodities
and not as natural resources to be exploited.

I have mentioned certain approaches to internal controls—self-
controls, if you will. They inhibit the free-swinging nature of
business in an effort to limit its excesses. Yet they pose a new
problem: How do you establish controls, whether from inside
or from outside, and preserve freedom?

Vitality and Morality

The proper balance between vitality and morality is most difficult
to locate. Conscience inevitably slows down action; responsibility
checks flexibility. How far, then, can business go in stressing the
moral factor? Psychologists warn us that too rigid or oppressive a
control of instinct is likely to devitalize a man. The rider must
certainly be in firm control; but if the horse is so whipped into

submission that it loses its spirit, it will never win any races for its rider. Likewise, it would be poor policy so to control business that it loses its drive. The so-called robber barons were examples of vitality with little or no control. However, if the vitality of business is overdisciplined, nothing of any significance—either good or bad—will be accomplished.

The search for a balance between freedom and responsibility which the businessman faces is somewhat more difficult than the equivalent search in other areas, and in our society as a whole. But its nature is the same. And in the great struggle for the hearts and minds of men our ability to strike a balance may be the deciding factor. If "freedom" means "excess" to the uncommitted millions who have yet to choose between Communism and democracy, they may well cast their lot on the side of "discipline" and "order."

The businessman has much to give to this common enterprise. If he can find an effective working balance in his own field, he will have made a decisive contribution to the total endeavor. But it is important that he recognize that he has a role of leadership to play in the over-all project as well. He is, in a real sense, teamed up with the doctor, the social worker, the government civil servant, the lawyer—and even the philosopher. All share in the benefits and the costs of our free, fluid, onrushing society; all must share in the continuing construction of a good—indeed, a better—society.

12.

The Psychology of Prosperity

By Ernest Dichter*

There is good evidence that prosperity is here to stay; still, one can clearly discern doubts and signs that the American people do not believe in the permanence of our present good luck. But what if we were never to be badly off again? What if things simply keep on getting better and better? It is my belief that learning to accept the permanent "burden" of a good life is one of the most challenging psychological problems of our age.

Probably for the first time in the history of the modern world, a country, the United States, has reached a point where most people have enough to eat and a good roof over their heads. Another aspect of human needs—personal recognition and human dignity—has also been achieved to a larger extent than ever before. The worker, ranging from handy man and plumber to farmer and white-collar worker, is proud of his occupation. He benefits by the existence of a labor market that makes his services available to only the highest bidder.

Thus, physical and social needs seem to have been widely fulfilled. Yet there is no doubt that the average American is far from being happy. There is still something missing in his life that he may never before have realized he needed. He has two cars in his garage, two or three television sets, and eats steak several times a week if he feels like it. Yet there is an over-all question in his

* Mr. Dichter is president of the Institute for Motivational Research, Inc.

mind which in the long run may make the difference between the perpetuation of our good life and its petering out. Where is he going? What is it all about?

He wants a clear definition of life. Maybe what he really wants is someone to tell him that it is really all right to lead a good life, to progress. Maybe he wants someone to give him a moral justification for not having to work any longer by the sweat of his brow.

But his need may go deeper. Perhaps what he seeks is a spiritual goal, using the word spiritual in its broadest sense. Several thousand years ago, when man was more fully aware of the fact that he does not live by bread alone, he searched for such spiritual definitions, possibly because they represented an escape from the miseries of everyday life. Most people did not have their physical needs satisfied and had no hope of ever eating enough and being really protected. It is only now, from a platform of satisfaction of worldly needs, that we can again approach the problem of spiritual goals.

*   *   *

An over-all definition of the meaning of life and the goals of humanity is not as complicated and frightening as it may sound at first. It is necessary to begin with biopsychological considerations. Once we are alive, we want to stay alive, in as undisturbed a fashion as possible; all our philosophies and morals are based on this desire. Death is the contradiction of growth; disease is the physical slowing down of parts or all of the body. All signs of deterioration are, in the biological sense, the antithesis of life and the beginning of death.

Yet we accept death only when it has actually occurred, and even then we try to find an explanation for it. We hardly ever are content with the statement, "He died." We almost always ask, "What did he die from?" as if knowing the cause could somehow make death appear as an accident which could have been avoided if we had only been more careful. In studies that we have done at the Institute for Motivational Research on the attitudes of Americans toward death, we found an almost humorous phrase continuously used—"if I die."

The physical, biological aspect of growth is paralleled by psychological growth. Here we are dealing with increasing maturity and independence as they occur under normal circumstances in the growth from child to adult. It can be defined like this: a life is the richer for the variety of experiences it can accumulate. These experiences may consist of adventure and travel, and they may range over thousands of miles; but new experiences may also be achieved within the limits of the physically narrow life, and in that case they would concern the development of insights, new understanding both of oneself and of other people.

In the broadest sense, psychological growth is the continuation of learning until the last day of one's life. It is comparable to the psychologist's concept of self-actualization—of realizing one's potentials—and it exists not only in the individual but also in humanity as a whole.

A society can be measured specifically on the basis of whether or not it contributes to and helps in self-actualization. Though we might state that a system is successful when it makes people happier, such a definition has very strong limitations. It is quite possible, for instance, that when living under a dictatorship some people are considerably happier than when living in a democracy. Yet dictatorship stunts psychological growth. We want happiness that is dynamic, not contented, cowlike happiness. Only the society which makes people happier in a dynamic sense by permitting them to live their lives in a fuller form, realizing the utmost potentialities of their own personalities, can be called a good society.

*   *   *

Physical needs can be defined and answered within the framework of one individual. Spiritual needs require the broader framework of the goals of humanity. Each individual can find fulfillment only by contributing his share to the fulfillment of the human race.

It seems to me that in the past many of our spiritual goals stemmed from immaturity in both the physical and the psychological sense. For instance, because people could not cope with life in the Middle Ages, they lived for the life hereafter—a way of thinking that persists in many subtle forms today. But since we are now reaching greater maturity in the economic and psychological senses, a new definition of spiritual goals may be necessary. The goal

setting may have to be done not only by those who have tradition-
ally done this job, such as the leaders of the church, but also by
businessmen.

The modern business executive is in a strategic position. He is a
natural leader in any effort to help revise and define the goals
sought by the individual and humanity. He has done his share
to help this country progress from old to new levels of maturity.
And through his direction of advertising, public relations, mer-
chandising, and other activities, as well as of company policy, he
plays a key role in influencing public opinion.

In revising our goals we will need to use concepts of maturity
and independence as criteria. Only those spiritual goals that help
people to become more independent and to realize their potentialities are right.

Thus, political democracy is worthwhile and ethical only if it
teaches and induces the citizen to become more and more an independent, self-reliant individual who accepts responsibility on
his own. How can we have a true government by the people if the
people themselves are not strong individuals, who have opinions
of their own and who can make decisions intelligently? The more
democracy is built on dependency of the father-image kind—
where decisions are referred to an all-powerful and almost superhuman president or statesman—the more we are violating the
basic goal of democratic procedures as well as spiritual goals.

Similarly, we must reject the image of a heavenly figure who
rewards and punishes daily conduct the way a father does. To the
extent that such an image leads to greater dependency on the part
of the individual and induces fatalistic attitudes, it becomes a
concept which, in a modern sense, is not only naïve but immoral.
How can a man's conduct be truly moral if it results from bribes
or threats rather than from responsible thought and self-willed
conviction?

In a memorable Broadway play, *The Lark,* by Jean Anouilh, the
Inquisitor, watching Joan of Arc being burned, says that what
made her really dangerous was not the fact that she had visions
but the fact that she had learned to trust in herself as a human
being. To discover that God was within her and had to be developed out of her own strength was true heresy in her time.

Today, Heidegger and other philosophers have introduced the concept of the growing God. God is not only the creator of the universe but the ideal to be reached within ourselves. If belief in God comprehends belief in one's self and the ability to grow and to realize one's potentialities, then indeed I think modern scientific psychological concepts and modern religious concepts find a complete relationship.

*   *   *

If the problem of defining new life goals is too big a one to be answered alone by philosophers and church leaders on Sunday mornings, then we must study it and help to solve it in our everyday lives.

While we are working on a job, the need for a goal definition is obscured. As long as we strive for the satisfaction of physical needs, we have little time to worry about spiritual ones. We can always utilize the illusion that we work in order to support our families, that work is a necessary evil and a duty. But this easy answer does not apply when we are confronted with more and more leisure time. Leisure time poses a grave threat. It will show up an empty life as lightning reveals an otherwise dark landscape.

We are caught in a cobweb of tradition and moral concepts which, starting with the idea of original sin, have portrayed life as a sequence of misery, worry, and toil. Prosperity as a corollary to a new kind of economy has started to make a big gaping hole in this web. Horatio Alger is thoroughly dead. Studies of college students show more and more that the desire for happiness and security, rather than the old "rags-to-riches" ideal, will determine the future of our young population. This philosophy is regrettable if it means the abandonment of the desire for growth and self-actualization. But if the argument of these young people is that foregoing exorbitant monetary rewards will permit them to come closer to the real goals of psychological growth, insight, and maturity, and thus happiness, this philosophy is a remarkable and fortunate development.

Many articles in management publications stress the fact that one of the biggest business problems we are faced with today is simply people. Incentive plans, decentralization, and management from the bottom up, all have been more or less successful attempts to cope with the restlessness of the Organization Man. The inadequacy of such methods may be that, while making the individual job more challenging, they do not meet the need for a new way of thinking about work—a new work culture, in other words.

Many companies have introduced music, gay colors, and so forth into industrial plants. They may consider these to be only gimmicks and smart employee-relations devices which give the appearance of making the working place a happier one. The true significance of these devices, however, is that they are the first break in the artificial separation between work and home, work and fun, work and the worthwhile aspects of life. We are witnessing only the beginning of the breakdown of these barriers. Advanced managements will do more and more in making the work place physically and psychologically indistinguishable from home.

So far, we still feel jittery and consider it almost criminal to give up even such minor symbols of the seriousness of work as the tie and jacket, and voluntary and involuntary disciplinary regulations. We still feel that we have to apply invisible whips in a multitude of forms to produce what we refer to as the work spirit. Moreover, the employee suffers from fears of incertitude if he stops feeling the whip; possibly, in fact, he may worry about it more than the employer. In some of my own studies, I have found that one of the most difficult tasks is to get an employee to forego reward and punishment systems and to substitute the acceptance of responsibility.

We all attempt to escape from freedom in our political, private, and job lives. At the same time, however, we are very slowly and gradually reaching a new level where it has become clear to us that the real salvation lies in greater maturity, greater acceptance of responsibility, and also a more reasonable attitude toward life, with fun and pleasure and happiness no longer considered immoral and unethical.

Over the last few decades we have witnessed a number of major revolutions in thinking. In the physical field, we have learned to accept the fact that it is not material or substance in its indivisible form that represents the building blocks of the world. Instead we have been forced to accept the frightening and almost incomprehensible idea (or so it may seem to the older generation) that this world is held together by electromagnetic forces of repulsion and attraction, that it consists of thousands of billions of electrons, protons, neutrons, all of them whirling around invisibly in all the things that we touch and deal with. This is an insight which is completely in contradiction to the tangible, physical world that our senses permit us to perceive.

Note that scientists were able to make this discovery only by abandoning, as misleading and erroneous, the dependence on empirical observations which Aristotle first demonstrated—only by substituting abstractions, by thinking in terms of electromagnetic wave lengths of five hundred or seven hundred meters. This was relatively easy to do in the physical world because the physicist had long ago established his right to approach the world in an objective and nonemotional fashion.

We have begun to witness a similar thought revolution in the field of biological sciences. Modern medicine cannot live any longer without the concepts of psychosomatic medicine. The fact that a cancer can be brought about not only by physiological and physical disturbances in the body, but also by a complex system of emotional disturbances translated into glandular and eventually into cellular disturbances, has been and is still frightening. An emotional disturbance and a neurosis cannot be observed through a microscope. Because of this, for many decades the so-called practical and empirically oriented scientists tried to deny the relationship of the emotions to the body.

The social sciences, too, are full of new discoveries, comparable to those in atomic physics and the field of biology. These discoveries seem to violate all common sense and direct observation, stipulated by Aristotle and others as the basis of scientific endeavor. The discovery of the unconscious, the acceptance of the flexibility of the human mind, Gestalt thinking, dynamic rather than static concepts—all are revolutionary in their implications. We are now seeing more and more the necessity of substituting a new kind of thinking to arrive at practical results. It is not easy. For example:

In advertising and public relations we are often confronted with the difficulty of shifting the attention of the top executive away from the concrete problems to the important ones tied in with a broader frame of reference. He often worries much more about what color to use in a particular advertisement and what language to use in describing his product than he worries about the corporate image, the company personality, the philosophy surrounding the use of a particular product, and other apparently intangible and nebulous factors which we have found are much more important in determining the success and failure of an advertising approach.

Similarly, to provide a man with a good job, to make his working conditions pleasant and give him recognition, we may need to do a good deal more in the way of relating work to the outside world and to humanity itself.

*   *   *

In some recent announcements the Soviet leaders have expressed their belief that they will achieve final victory by means of out-producing us in every field. Even there, though, they have learned that efficient production is based to a large extent on the psychological practice of morale and incentives. If we are to maintain our superiority, we must pay more attention to the morale problem of the individual employee and the nation as a whole. What I am suggesting does not mean an increased paternalism where the executive starts worrying about the spiritual satisfactions of his employees. Instead, in line with our previous discussion, the answer lies in the exact opposite direction.

The American executive has an important job in helping his staff and employees grow as mature individuals and in stimulating them toward increased independence. But often, when he has reached a certain degree of financial security and looks around for lofty goals, he becomes interested in charity, politics, and various other occupations. Instead of seeking such satisfactions on the outside, might he not do well to devote more "missionary" work to his own organization? I suggest that in many instances the very same needs which push him in idealistic directions exist among his employees, as they in turn reach the greater financial security that goes along with prosperity.

In other words, to be realistic we shall have to consider that the real test of the efficiency of an organization lies more and more in whether or not the individual employees have grown not only financially and socially but also in maturity. An organization has failed, despite rising sales and profits, if this maturing process has not taken place. Incentive and profit-sharing plans are the financial tools with which this can be achieved. What is needed are the psychological corollaries of such plans.

Emotional growth does not take place overnight in an organization. Senior executives must experience it before they can effectively set up systematic procedures, psychological techniques of encouragement and insight, and so on for the benefit of others. More important than anything else, emotional growth is affected by the general attitudes which are permitted to prevail within an organization. The development of maturity is not an easy test for a company to meet, but it is a very significant one. It not only affects business performance, but in the last analysis it is the basis for the success of our democratic procedures and thus our whole way of life.

This book may be kept

FOURTEEN DAYS

A fine will be charged for each day the book is kept overtime.

Jul 27 '64			
Apr 27 67			
May 10 67			
SEP 1 1 1979			